Creativity

Nature and Us

Exploring Green Themes
through the Arts

Bo Jeffares Sekine

British Library Cataloguing in Publication Data:
A catalogue record for this book is available from the British Library

ISBN: 978-0-9935040-0-6

First published 2016 by Bo's Books

Cover: selection from a landscape collection; each image 168 x 116 cm
Sky, Sea and Land/Crop Circles/Moon Reflected on Still Water/
Yin Yang Landscape/Water/Red Italy

Please see www.bojeffaressekine.co.uk

Image of René Magritte's The Healer (Le Thérapeute), 1937
© ADAGP, Paris and DACS, London 2015

Use of images of The Spinners by Diego Rodriguez de Velazquez,
Detail of Journey of The Magi by Benozzo Gozzoli,
Allegory by Giovanni Bellini, with thanks to Getty Images

Printed and bound by TJ International, Padstow, Cornwall

Bo Jeffares Sekine, Garden

Dedication

This book is for everyone. Everyone is an earth artist. Everyone pictures ways to translate ideas into actions.

My thanks go to Andy Goldsworthy, Charles Jenks, Richard Lang, Richard Long and Peter Randall-Page for the kind inclusion of their images, and also to all those who have helped me throughout my life.

Contents

How this Book Evolved

How do we form our relationship with Mother Earth?

This question lies at the heart of this book. Like me it has evolved like a snail. It explores two loves: art and nature. I have painted and drawn since I can remember, inspired by nature's colour and beauty. As a young child in Australia I was fascinated by dazzling exotic flowers, scented trees and intricate shell shapes. I became increasingly intrigued by nature's varied interactions and our own contributions to this complex game.

In ancient Greece and Renaissance Italy scientific enquiry and aesthetic excellence went hand in hand. Not so when I was young. As I took arts subjects I was not allowed to study biology. So I compensated by exploring plant remedies, practical gardening, and cultural traditions which interpret nature intuitively, such as Chinese Taoism and the Aboriginal concept of Dream Time.

Starting to weave complimentary interests together, seeking holistic harmonies, I first sought areas where art and literature cross-fertilise. I studied fine art, art history and art criticism, and wrote a book examining the role of artists in fiction. Later, given a chance to write on European landscape painting, I wondered how we all relate to landscape. How do we feel about the earth? Why do we adapt earthly scenery to express imaginative ideas about heaven and hell? This universal theme is explored more fully here. Why do we project ideas of perfection into so many media, including pictures, poems, parks, gardens, films, photographs and earth art? Earth artists highlight wild sites and rearrange organic materials to publicise private concerns about the environment. We all adapt the arts while trying to express our evolving relationships with the earth.

Emotional connections with the land are strong, although we are sometimes unaware of our exact responses and their resultant consequences. As our impact is frequently lethal we are necessarily becoming more self-aware. Reflecting on what the earth means to us individually we frequently fine-tune our thought processes as we evolve into new caretakers rather than old exploiters.

Having lived and worked in Japan and been lucky enough to visit some Zen gardens, I wanted to explore an East/West polarity. Staged, spatial experiments exploited by Tea House architects lead the mind from the mundane to the marvellous. Where else can we find artistic works which move us from everyday spaces to evocations of the infinite?

A dextrous writer and a subtle visual artist achieve this from a European standpoint. *The Tempest* by Shakespeare and *The Spinners* by Velasquez illustrate how spatial imagery can entice our imagination away from hard facts to creative dreams. Art works can help us to expand or dissolve old mental boundaries. Modern quantum physics reiterates the wisdom of ancient mystics suggesting constant flux or interchange between solids and vibrations, seen and unseen worlds, an eternal dance between matter and energy.

We all deal in invisible energy all the time. We 'send love'. We get 'hunches'. We use electricity, try acupuncture and intuitively guess who is about to phone us. We generate thoughts and feelings like little power stations. Largely intangible (unless you hook up to a competent brain scanner or brilliant telepath) our potent 'brain waves' are high energy sources. We are, therefore, all creators, all contributors to the universal energy field, all responsible for the planet's welfare, as our ideas feed into actions.

Some art tries to shock, scare and confuse. Some is cold, impersonal and mechanised. But celebratory art constantly makes 'good medicine'. Optimistic imagery provides a positive charge, contributing to the universal feel good factor. Whether deeply sensitive or deceptively casual, positive pictures provide heart-warming catalysts. Samuel Palmer's harvest moons illuminate rich fertile fields to evoke nature's intangible mysteries. Matisse's palmate leaves bounce about amongst his stars and flowers to evoke nature's abundance with jazzy joy. Both work.

Immense and minute aspects of nature can connect visually to link cells and stars, microcosms and macrocosms. In sacred geometry, whether Celtic or Classical, circles represent completed lifecycles and emotional fulfilment. Circles can fuse old visions of earthly playgrounds with new ecological advances to help germinate new seed thoughts.

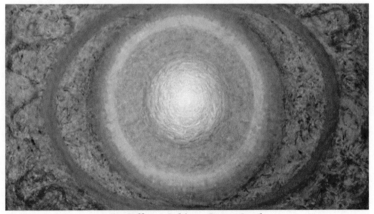

Bo Jeffares Sekine, Green Seed

How many world religions envisage heaven as a perfect place? Heavenly harmony is traditionally expressed through control of the elements within an idealised or geometric composition. As a young student I created an abstract paradise place: this early environmental had a central tree of life and a fountain of wine. Its scarlet and blue floor pattern was reproduced on a small game board, anticipating a curiosity about life games.

Exhibiting landscapes internationally, I have tried to create colourful pictures to capture the essence of land, sea and sky, creating distilled catalysts for meditation. These peaceful paintings are interspersed with energy splashes of pollen, fire or water. Calm images of open vistas, luminous skies and empty beaches antidote overdoses of technology and industrialisation.

Colours are vital, like emotional foods. They stabilise or energise. They create moods. Imagine eating grey strawberries or watching a beige sunset? Would you? Hot suns are both physically and emotionally warming. Cool moons pull our oceans and inspire poetic reflection. Our physical environment provides a shared global language. Roads help us to map our physical journeys and also to plot metaphysical 'life paths'. Fertile fields, where we successfully cultivate food for survival, are adapted to suggest other fruitful interactions with nature.

Beautiful landscapes, such as those in Cornwall which combine wild scenery and artistic interpretation, provide valuable cultural deposits within our memory banks. Creating mental blueprints, we move thoughts and feelings through spoken and written words into concrete form. The expression 'Carbon Footprints', for example, demonstrates us processing change at an ideas level. Bare-footed ancestors left their footprints on local ground. Now we start to realise that we influence the whole planet all the time. Carbon

Footprints refer to our polluting presence to increase a shared 'ground of understanding' and promote environmental awareness.

But are footprints made of carbon? No. But by bringing scientific information down-to-earth, by fusing it with our own body language, we clarify a global problem. Each person and each footprint is unique. So by blending the impersonal element of 'carbon' (for the way we poison the earth's atmosphere) with the image of individual 'footprints' we create a composite metaphor. We encapsulate a shared challenge and personal responsibility.

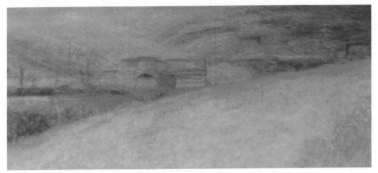

Bo Jeffares Sekine, Detail, Farm and Field

'Down-to-earth' doesn't imply leaping head first into a red hot volcano but common sense, practical wisdom, being securely grounded in heart and mind. Common proverbs and popular phrases illustrate how we continually adapt landscape imagery in everyday conversation. The word 'earth' means planet or soil. Sometimes these two ideas become interchangeable. We continually juggle themes and meanings, concepts and visions. Nature provides the matrix, or the raw materials for these experiments, the results of each person's inner growth, the flowering of their creative minds. As John Updike said 'any activity becomes creative when the doer cares about doing it right or better.'

So imaginative food for thought generates food for survival.

Trees of Life

Trees, symbolising growth, provide a constant theme linking art works worldwide. Easy to see, and touch, they provide strong images. These are also easy to adapt aesthetically. The human condition, including branching vascular and neural patterns, is reflected in such visualisations. Words, pictures, sculpture, land art, gardening and interwoven landscaping processes are inspired by our age-old fascination with symbolic Trees of Life. Healthy, balanced roots and branches evoke balanced social systems and organisations, as well as inspiring balanced personal growth.

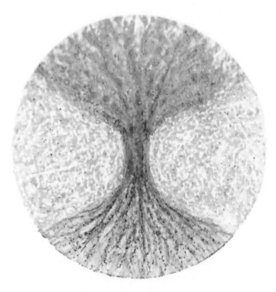

Bo Jeffares Sekine, Roots and Branches

Natural scenery, once something in the background of our lives (and our image-making) has been steadily coming forward both in the mind's eye, and in our material reckoning. As forests are wiped out on a regular basis with no thought for the future, woods which were once taken for granted now become prized out of all recognition.

Landscape, traditionally plundered and polluted, now has a new name – the environment. This word carries new connotations. Our environment is something to be conserved, cherished and protected. No longer just a picturesque backdrop to everyday lives and actions, the earth is finally appreciated as the very warp and weft of our continued existence.

We are becoming increasingly aware of our duties of care towards a unique world. We see the Earth from the lenses of cameras outside our protective atmosphere, so we gain an objective appreciation of the fragility of this intricate planet. We become increasingly aware of the responsibilities we carry for mental attitudes and their inevitable materialisations. Changing attitudes can be sensed through artists' antics. International artworks mirror our approaches to Mother Earth. They focus on precarious situations and can help to promote positive changes.

We use key aspects of our environment to express our fundamental attitudes to life. 'Every cloud has a silver lining' is a thought-provoking example. There is a constant interplay between landscape and life. The Bible, for example, speaks tellingly of people in anguish experiencing 'the valley of the shadow of death' and 'the dark night of the soul'.

Literature reflects this creative interchange. Shakespeare deftly evokes the 'winter of our discontent'. Weather and climatic change express the human condition, as when we feel 'under the weather' or suffer from 'fair weather' friends. Shakespeare also memorably equates love with seasonal perfection: 'Shall I compare thee to a summer's day? Thou art more temperate and more beautiful'.

Trees represent organic life. Balanced root and branch systems link earth and sky, connecting sunlight with soil. Anchored in the ground, absorbing moisture and nutrients, growing into the air and interacting with the sun our trees photosynthesise to keep the planet green and our atmosphere healthy. They prevent erosion. They temper planetary winds. They contribute homes, building materials, foods, medicines and visual delights.

Bo Jeffares Sekine, Walled Garden

Bo Jeffares Sekine, Blue Winter

Trees are an eternal symbol of life. They have inspired whole communications systems. According to legend, the Norse god Odin hung upon the great tree of life for nine days and nights. When twigs fell off to spell out formulas and words, creating the runic alphabet, each symbol was frequently associated with a specific tree.

Trees are used to evoke endless structures and situations, as with Darwin's famous sketch of an evolutionary tree, or indeed everyone's genetic family tree. Electricians place tree symbols on earth wires to indicate safety. Statisticians enliven their structural analyses with references to organic 'branches,' while computer scientists work with what they describe as 'rooted tree' graphs.

Tree imagery inspires descriptions of books and bodies. We ourselves can be read 'like an open book'. On meeting new people we will try not to 'judge a book by its cover'. The pages of this book can be referred to as leaves. And we say we'll 'take a leaf out of someone's book' or decide to 'turn over a new leaf'. We continually 'branch out' as we create new experiences. The structure holding both of us together is called a spine – whether for a leaf or a human body. We, like trees, have central trunks. We sport limbs, have veins, pores, cuticles, root chakras and stem cells. We exfoliate!

Landscape architects play on these parallel systems. The versatile garden designer Maggie Keswick created red and blue streams to symbolise our branching veins and arteries. Paul Klee earlier compared an artist's life with that of a tree's organic growth. Just as the tree draws up nutrients from the earth below, so the artist attempts to transform worldly information into inspirational beauty. Klee thought that individual artists acted as tree trunks, intuitively processing information for all their contemporaries.

Our bodies and faces symbolically express our reactions. We 'face facts' logically, or 'face the music' emotionally. And now, moving from social situations to mechanical manufacture, we become adept at creating technical 'interfaces' and forming Face Books.

Links between human forms and earthly landscape are endless. The ancient Chinese, for example, equated mountains with bones. Rounded hills in pairs suggested breasts. Land and women are described as barren or fertile. Grass, in the Japanese tradition, can be equated poetically with the growing hair of the dead. Walt Whitman takes up this Eastern theme in verses playing with the continuous energy flow between people and places. Why should a motorway have a hard shoulder? This image illustrates how archetypal links between people and natural structures are updated as technology develops, and 'hard facts' softened by being given more familiar human attributes.

Traditional agrarian boundaries such as wooded hedges (which also allow us to protect, or to hedge, our bets) are being updated by sophisticated bankers creating flexible 'hedge funds'. Trees inspire 'trunk' roads in transport systems, and 'branch' lines are small offshoots of railway networks. Similarly, a 'branch' can refer to a minor office, shop, bank or indeed any secondary business or commercial venture. The Root and Branch Bill, passed by the British government in the 19th century referred, hopefully, to an all encompassing system of social and political reform.

We employ landscape terms to define human qualities and endeavours. We can be stuck in a cleft stick. We can touch wood for luck. We can see people as chips off the old block. Concise thought is neatly expressed in a nut shell.

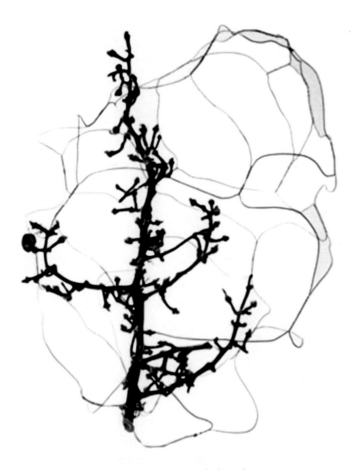

Bo Jeffares Sekine, Seed Thought

Seed thoughts are frequently coloured by a country's native flora and fauna. The slow growing oak, which provides a safe home for many species in England, generates a strong cultural train of thought. It represents moral value and personal reliability. Traditionally worshipped by druids in oak groves, these sturdy trees still provide a rich national chain of reference through linked proverbs, literature and conversation.

There are romantic stories of folk heroes safely concealed in dense, leafy oaks. These strong trees were valued by successive generations of artists, poets and craftsmen. Oaks were equally cherished by native architects and ship builders relying on their wood to create long – lasting buildings and to prepare seaworthy sailing ships for protection, trade and exploratory adventures.

Popular proverbs such as 'from little acorns great oaks grow,' express wisdom in colloquial, everyday terms.

Shakespeare praises his resilient countrymen's 'hearts of oak.' Similarly, Frenchmen refer to a beautiful woman as *'une belle plante'*, whilst wives of well secured husbands confirm that they are *'bien planté'*. Such themes are constant. Buddhists believe that everyone contains potential seeds of perfection. Ideas germinate, plans grow, talents blossom (or are nipped in the bud), beauties bloom, labours bear fruit and time itself becomes 'ripe'.

Who can fail to understand a politician asserting he works at grassroots level, or a gardener having green fingers, or a guerrilla gardener launching seed bombs? Our links with the landscape are expressed in many metaphors. We seek the root of a problem. When shattered, we are shaken to the core. When secure, we take root, or describe ourselves as safely rooted in reality. Conversely, cut off from security by travelling or being homeless we become rootless. *Déraciné* was the French term Buckminster Fuller used to describe his artist friend Isamu Noguchi, born part American and part Japanese.

Even a worm can turn. Landscape terminology expresses personal and professional facts. See Shakespeare's observation: 'Here come two religious caterpillars'. The animal kingdom provides us with a rich vein of comparative pickings. We can be as brave as a lion, cunning as a fox, sick as a parrot, or in Australian parlance have a kangaroo loose in our top paddock. Social instincts are expressed by proverbs such as 'birds of a feather' flock together, or loners appear like 'fish out of water'.

Water and other elements are adapted to suggest character, as with descriptions of fiery temperaments or vague air heads. Native American names reflected strongly sensed links with the landscape. Adopted names can be ironic as with blues singer Muddy Waters. Insights into personalities are evoked by phrases such as still waters run deep, or telling references to winds of change. Time and tide wait for no man.

Punning, playing with words, keeps poets in business. Seeking and revealing eternal truths, they reveal the universal within the particular. They transmute personal pain and private pleasure into universal currency. This alchemical process crystallises the underlying unity between us and All-That-Is. Poetry illustrates such eternal energies at work, whether christened Chi by the Chinese or the Life Force by Westerners such as the Irish playwright George Bernard Shaw.

Dylan Thomas, a poet with a good bouncy imagination, fused electrical power with the colour green: 'The force that through the green fuse drives the flower/Drives my green age.' Love and landscape are all the same for Thomas who mixes sex and sites to produce poetical pictures in *Under Milk Wood* (1954). He makes lyrical links between people and places, playing with the word 'bed', equally applicable for plants or lovers, 'Chasing the naughty couples down the grassgreen gooseberried double bed of the wood.'

Nurseries also provide similar linguistic parallels. They describe sites for new stars, for nurturing young seedlings or human babies.

Similarly, human organs and green seedlings are both 'transplanted'. Architecture is adapted to express social situations. Young people decide to go 'up the housing ladder'. Career women 'hit glass ceilings.' Builders materialise or 'fleshout' or 'carcass' structures.

In *Feng Shui,* the Chinese art of optimising all spatial potential, windows are equated with eyes. Windows let in light. They also provide views of the outside world. Windows therefore combine physical and metaphysical meanings. They can also be opened in physical or metaphysical ways, as when we consult our latest technology seeking new 'windows of opportunity'.

Natural themes reoccur as we reflect on our interactions with our environment. We create imaginative scenery to express our inner feelings. Landscape was always revered in Eastern art, but in the West was once confined to a few tasteful twigs, or a chunk of cloud behind the head of some favourite saint or mistress. But scenery gradually came into its own to become valued as a source of creative inspiration.

Landscape painting gradually became a distinct painterly category. It was one up from still life but still several grades down from so-called thinking, or intellectual art, such as the serious to dull depiction of historical or philosophical subjects. This of course was ludicrous, but goes to show how far we have moved on, gradually adapting our attitude to our surroundings and resultant depictions of nature.

In the Renaissance an archetypal Road of Life theme was popular with important royal and religious patrons. *The Journey of the Magi* (1459-61) depicted the journey of the three kings of Orient following a star to seek the infant Jesus. This naturally allowed for some landscape background.

The progress of these sages inspired a colourful work by Gozzoli. In his meticulous image there are richly detailed and decorative trees along a winding route. But such carefully constructed landscape features, however delightful, were a secondary factor. This approved quest conformed to contemporary standards. Medici princes are depicted on an esoteric pilgrimage, portrayed in the prestigious role of 'wise men'. This commission, like modern advertising projects, was designed to bestow prestige on keynote 'travellers', ostensibly upgrading contemporary magnates to a more spiritual realm.

Benozzo Gozzoli, The Journey of the Magi

Rich patrons adore flattery. So within the context of Roads of Life, Gozzoli was paid to promote his patrons' power rather than to evoke planetary appreciation.

Compare the inspiration behind this early image with the way a much later land artist, Andy Goldsworthy, plays with natural paths and streams to produce his personally motivated artworks.

Goldsworthy selects real leaves and genuine flowers to compose his simple and memorable designs and progressions. He photographs organic constructions capturing their intrinsic beauties. In so doing he highlights nature's ephemeral transitions.

Gardens and Galleries

How did nature regain respect?
How did artists gain freedom for personal expression?
How did their relationship with the earth evolve?

The dissolution of feudal landholding was a movement whereby control of the land by churches and nobles was reflected by a parallel loss of control over visual imagery. There was more democratic land use and ownership, and landscape painting also became revered as a subject its own right. The land became cherished for its visual qualities. Landscapes became vehicles for complex studies of light and shade and subtle attempts to capture atmosphere.

One of the indications of this slow development can be seen in artists seeking social prestige and increasing creative independence. They started to take responsibility for choosing their own themes and marketing their own works. More came to have private patches of land. There is a shining popular example of just such an independent artist. Monet, the Impressionist, was a man who, once established, refused to send pictures to his dealer in Paris, until he himself felt completely ready to part with them. This artist was a man who, by his own admission, had as many seed as paint catalogues scattered throughout his home. He loved his garden. It kept him going in hard times, inspired his images, and remains a magnet for aesthetes worldwide.

In Giverny, Monet was not just painting landscape but creating it. He paid a lot of attention to detail. He had arguments with small-minded local dignitaries to increase his water supply. He contrived a careful collection of plants – juxtaposing old and new imported species. His walkways, famous wisteria bridge and abundance of seasonal blooms became a complementary form of expression. Garden features fed his painterly eye, as his love of colour and the filtering effects of sunlight through foliage and water inspired the materialisation of his luminous water lily images.

Monet blurred creative categories. He fused garden design with painting. He had equal success in both fields. Other artists also started to explore new areas of overlap between picture-making and landscape appreciation. Many reflected the spirit of the places they loved most, the *genus loci* of favourite sites. It is hard to look at a later Mondrian, for example, without subconsciously recalling the strict linear divisions and flat colour fields produced by Dutch bulb growers. His rectangular compositions also pay tribute to the geometrical layout of New York City. His late-night, deep blue, light-spattered, jazz-inspired Broadway Boogie-Woogie (1942–3) fuses feeling with form.

Some artists know what has inspired them, and can say so directly – as with Constable's famous remarks about absorbing realistic local details, such as old rotting posts, during his boyhood by the River Stour. These formed his painterly concerns, instigated his pictorial vocabulary. Other painters seem less consciously aware of their inspiration or, indeed, their whole creative process.

Take the case of Patrick Heron. Once he was able to leave London as an independent painter he returned to Cornwall where he had lived as a child. Heron instinctively sought an isolated house, two hundred metres up above the Atlantic, named Eagle's Nest, which he had earlier known and come to love.

Bo Jeffares Sekine, Paradise Garden

Heron entitled some of his abstracts 'garden paintings'. This painter spent much of his free time working in his windswept wild garden. It had been formed by an earlier artist, and consisted of natural boulders left *in situ* with exotic bushes and plants creating garden rooms linked by curving paths. Heron shaped these spaces against the wind's ravages. When he grew successful as an artist a partial retrospective was organized. He was taken up in a helicopter for a spin, as part of the nonsense accompanying his fame, and did he get a shock.

As they floated around, rising and falling, he was 'utterly astonished. There below me, in plan, were all my recent gouaches'. These had been entirely non-figurative, even though he had subconsciously called them 'garden gouaches'. Heron admits that any artist's creations mirror their obsessions. He states that his own particular abstract vision was to produce endless versions of a 'square-round' theme. 'I found myself gazing into a dense tapestry of area-shape images, all dovetailed, all mutually defining each other as colour-shapes, exactly as identical shapes behave in my paintings.' He had thus provided a case, as Herbert Read would have said, of art equalling 'pattern informed by sensibility'.

Whilst Heron clipped bushes unselfconsciously, Gertrude Jekyll (who once lived in a cottage next door to him) evolved during her life from painting to garden design. She defined landscaping as 'painting a landscape with living things.' 'No artificial planting can ever equal that of nature' said Jekyll. She began her career embroidering dandelions in the William Morris style, was later lovingly referred to by her architect friend Lutyens as the 'Mother of All Bulbs'. She could complement his architectural, hard edged creations with soft, romantic plantings. Jekyll was practical. She could make a dry stone wall. She was also acutely aware of the pleasures of informal borders and gently orchestrated colour gradations. She was responsible for trying to combine buildings and gardens into unified aesthetic statements.

A subsequent husband and wife team Geoffrey and Susan Jellicoe also enhanced this creative field. Geoffrey made the history, design, and aesthetics of landscape architecture an internationally viable subject. His wife was set to work selecting suitable plants for specific sites. They, too, helped to blur boundaries defining fine and landscape arts.

Monet made a garden which seeded garden paintings, marrying twin obsessions. Heron experienced a 'shock of recognition' on seeing how his gardening had inspired his pictures. Other independent artists turned patches of land into virtual galleries. Starting to dispense with middlemen and gallery owners, creators increasingly present and market their own creations.

Henry Moore, for example, used the countryside around his house to show his work in his own specific way. He bought up land in spectacular fashion to site individual pieces in selected places. His huge stone and metal creations were placed in natural contexts which he felt showed them off to their best advantage. This was no case of daintily moving maquettes on shelves, but dropping boulders into fields. Starting with no money, he gradually built up a seventy acre property. He created a factory with nine studios adapted for sculpture making with varied materials. Conserving age-old hedges and building a small mound (like a Neolithic tomb) to act as a viewing platform, he set about directing operations to display his huge, three-dimensional works to his own satisfaction. He was in charge, he set the scene.

He felt that some of his smooth, simplistic sculptures were best appreciated on a lawn, or beside a pool, whilst others might be 'more effective' or 'more poignant' set against the rhythm and raggedness of tree branches. Others required a secret glade hidden by high foliage to foster privacy. *Family Group* (1945–9) a monumental composite of linked male, female and infant figures as pared down and effective as an Etruscan bronze, was set in a field of flax as blue as summer skies.

This sculptor's profound feelings for nature – 'enough inspiration for two million years' – inspired his creation of an 'open' garden designed to 'almost' merge with its surroundings. Moore had a great sense of satisfaction when natural forces affected his work, as when sheep accidentally rubbed up against a vast piece to affect its patina. He experienced a deep sense of distraction or loss when a piece was removed from one of his chosen rural settings.

This was surely part and parcel of an overall attitude? His first source of inspiration had been a bleak lump of stone surrounded by gnarled trees. Moore's overall aim was to open people's eyes, and to help them to increase their overall sensitivity to 'life and nature'.

Another, extremely different, artist – many of whose works can hardly be separated from their landscape sites – was Ian Hamilton Finlay. This Scot, who employed numerous artists and craftsmen to materialise his ideas, was a concrete poet. On a bit of windswept Scottish moorland he planted a selection of sculptural conceits; both slight and serious.

Et in Arcadia Ego and his classically provocative *See Poussin, Hear Lorraine* remain timeless. This oblique reference, elegantly inscribed on a stone plaque, places his living sanctuary in a direct line with early, idealising masters. Poussin and Lorraine, the first formal, the second lyrical, were traditional paradise painters. Both evoked their ideals through adaptations of natural scenery making mindscapes for future generations.

Eco-architects try to create heaven on earth with their practical skills. Theoretical values are combined with horticultural knowledge, plus hopes for self-sufficiency and local food production. Trapping sun light, using geothermal or wind power, collecting rainwater, planting reed beds, many also envisage planting directly in and around their constructions carpeting them with trees and foliage. Ken Yeang, born in Malaysia, based in Britain, working in Singapore is one such architect. In this self-consciously landscaped city, gardening is an integral part of planning regulations, an enforced legal requirement. High rise buildings include public 'sky parks'. Huge edifices display 'living walls' like so many updated versions of the famous hanging gardens of Babylon.

Bo Jeffares Sekine, Trees on a Skyscraper

Yeang deftly fuses trees with a tower. *Fusionopolis* is designed with a vertical spine of planting rising up through a fifteen storey building. This green design practically cools and insulates, and also harmonises the emotional energies of those inhabiting his architectural designs. Bridging the gap between plants and people, international minds like his learn from photosynthesising by transforming light into energy.

Trees and shrubs could be the tallest elements on a *Garden Bridge* proposed for London's river Thames. Natural planting, trees, slugs and curving paths will try to combat stress by deliberately slowing people down. Most bridges are built for speed and access. This reversal is another sign of people starting to value nature, and its beauty, as much or more than utilitarian convenience. Thomas Heatherwick (having made a *Seed Cathedral* in 2010) is now working out how to 'give love' to two sterile urban spaces. In theory his living bridge can link them to let urban travellers relax as they travel.

Enclosed Paradises – Dissolving Boundaries

Fear encloses. Hope enlarges. Many mental and physical boundaries were broken in the nineteenth century. When Monet and his colleagues started to produce what were then considered incredibly slap-dash, unprofessional pictures, critical contemporaries ridiculed them as mere 'impressions'. Not only was 'proper' landscape painting a more precise and meticulous affair, but photography which is now so popular was also highly suspect. Artists like Ingres or Corot used it to experiment, to steal ideas, perhaps to save time and cash for models and trips. But officially, photography was still deemed an inferior art form, quite unable to compete with the official hierarchy of Fine Arts.

Now things are different. This turnabout was recorded by London's Tate Modern. When it first opened its doors a Monet painting of reflections of light on water, set in a luxuriant gold frame, was revered by a public who now approached it as an Old Master. Monet's technical subtlety and evocative grace shone out against a rough contrast. Richard Long's irregular rock circle proved that landscape imagery has a power of its own.

Sir Nicholas Serota, summing up Long's impact in 'Heaven and Earth' his exhibition at Tate Modern in 2009, writes that few artists can 'make us more aware of both the power and the fragility of the earth or, indeed, of our own brief passage across its face'.

Earth art, like Long's, can include stark stones, a throwback to our Neolithic past minus early social or psychic connections. Land art is also revered in photographs, as with the Tate's early choice of an image of earth and rock uncovered at an archaeological site.

As there are no limits or rules in the art world now, so resultant works can either reflect freedom of expression, or the creation of more of the Emperor's New Clothes. David Hockney serves up composite shots, sometimes tongue-in-cheek, as when he plays on photographic clichés, like tourists recording 'been there, done that'. This versatile, technically adventurous artist uses his own camera to record a visit to a Japanese landscape garden. Later he paints round the border of his photograph. He adds footprints, signs of his own transient visit to a specific site. Hockney presents such photographs as art works in their own right. The Japanese garden which he photographs forms his central image. The pseudo naïve footprints, which he paints around its border, symbolise his own walk around its perimeters, a jokey image of a personal journey.

Social boundaries dissolving since medieval times have parallels in the corresponding dissolution of barriers within the art world. Landscape, once a set vehicle for expressing heaven and hell ('float or roast') often described fixed celestial and infernal territories. Moral boundaries between good and evil were reflected in physical boundaries; divisions between earth and sky. Now they become increasingly flexible as we make up our own minds on so many issues. Art adjusts as we experiment to define personal ideals.

Look, for example, at mediaeval and early Renaissance paradise gardens. The *hortus conclusus* or enclosed garden, was just that – enclosed. Its walls were definite boundaries.

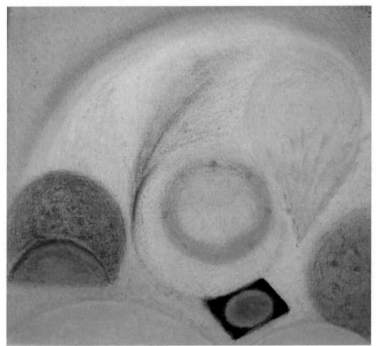

Bo Jeffares Sekine, Detail, Enclosed Garden/Playground

Such gardens were encapsulated by tight fences, adorned with neatly pruned roses. Rich gold leaf blanked out the distance. Or there was no distance. It was not encouraged. Limiting factors within the then Church may have wished to focus attention on the organisation's material and worldly power rather than encouraging freedom of religious thought, more modern direct-line spirituality. Curiosity and questioning could be dangerous. Early paradise gardens reflected fears of nature and of the unknown. Caged minds create caged images. Early paradises were gilded cages.

Go a step further and look at Bellini's *Sacred Allegory,* a touchstone in Western ideal landscapes. Bellini, advocate of spiritual surrealism, opens out the original *hortus conclusus*, or enclosed paradise. He presents an allegorical comment on, or description of, a perfect environment, producing an ageless masterpiece.

Bellini evokes a sophisticated game plan. The Virgin is relegated to the side of the overall composition. A tree of life, neatly potted, occupies his central stage. The characters he places on his geometric floor remain static, fixed in time. The main interest lies not in them individually or collectively but in a linked expanse of opening landscape.

Giovanni Bellini, Sacred Allegory

This is an elegant vista, a perfect evocation of calm and content, earthly and idealistic. Bellini not only allows us to see it through the wide spaces between the uprights of his symbolic partition, but also through his central, open gate. This is a breakthrough. We are visually encouraged to look out and to explore. This is a generous invitation. Our eyes automatically move out over his clear blue water plane to savour a tantalising view which combines wild and formal elements. This is landscape painting at its most profound. There is a mysterious, unfathomable quality infused throughout this whole image. 'If I could say it, I wouldn't paint it', Bellini implies. Like Giorgione, at his best producing the poetic delights of *The Tempest*, Bellini leaves a subtle aftershock, not so much an earthquake more a blessing.

Where Bellini is peaceful, wise and ultimately reassuring, Magritte is cool, detached and cynical. A modern surrealist master, or calculating anarchist, he has not only opened gates but mentally kicked us through them.

We are in unknown territory. His surrealism is not spiritual, but existential. His experiments with sky and space (joking with gravity, along with sexual taboos and any other conventional formats) make him like a Zen teacher, teaching by provocation. He supplies paradoxes. He makes us reconsider established, conventional positions. He breaks every barrier he can by reversing archetypal imagery. Surely his wisdom lies in his absurdity?

Magritte, playing with scale and technique, adapted tricks of overlap and textural contrast experimented with in collage. He places an object or person in, or on, a totally illogical environment, fabricating a landscape of the absurd. His air is full of floating rocks. His clouds are hard as nails. Yet for all his ironic detachment, it may be significant that as he got older he wrote to a friend to say that he had decided to cut down on prolific experiment for the sake of it and wanted to concentrate on fewer, more carefully selected images, which he knew would have a studied impact.

So what did he choose? Magritte had made many ingenious experiments with trees. He produced his own advertising pictures of tree trunks cut open to reveal a specific product. *Le Dernier Cri* (1967) shows a last variation on his early leaf trees. Finally, this great experimenter decided to restate an archetypal symbol, the universal tree of life.

Where Magritte was cool, Matisse was hot. This dazzling, sensual colourist also cut down to the same concluding image. When he made his late Oceana images, he avoided a set or limiting horizon. He created cut-outs to present a melodious image of nature, floating seas or skies decorated with birds and fishes. These were linked by his visual shorthand for vegetal growth.

Simplified palmate leaves, like pieces of seaweed, characterise his late works – such as the stained glass lighting his chapel at Venice. When asked whether he believed in God, he replied: 'I do when I'm working' equating spirituality with expression.

Compare the enormous simplicity of these two artists' final works, reducing the tree of life into abstract forms. This is the force of modern minimalism. Hundreds of years away from Gozzoli's gilded lollipop trees, they speak directly to everyone like children's art, so often the simpler the better.

Matisse's abstract leaf or seaweed shape is a classic, easily absorbed as a sign of growth. Some artists express a fascination with symbols which can be read in several ways. Magritte, for example, sometimes adapted the wider part of his leaf trees into birds' bodies. Bellini had earlier placed a centaur, part man/part beast, on the right hand side of his allegorical vista. This centaur symbolically links man with the animal world to represent Bellini's love of classical culture to enrich Christian beliefs.

Myths about metamorphosis, bridging the gaps between man and nature, are particularly potent involving trees. Take the Daphne myth, for example, where a fleeing girl is transformed into a tree. Bernini's marble version of Daphne is unsurpassed. He renders each area of transformation in marble. Toes turn to roots, fingers to foliage. His baroque subtlety, contrasting smooth skin with rough bark remains a *tour de force*.

Bo Jeffares Sekine, Leaves

But Matisse is equally poignant. He spent hours and hours drawing, and editing until he reached a point of apparent naïvety as in *The Dance* (1910). But if you copy his simplistic sketches they often look odd. This master of direct reduction linked person and plant by making a sketch of one of Picasso's lovers as a flower.

Bo Jeffares Sekine, Plant People

Frieda Kahlo was another artist intrigued by the vegetal world. She painted a portrait of herself and her parents with their feet firmly planted in the soil. This exotic Mexican painter's portrait of Luther Burbank provides another intriguing figure within this genre. Burbank was a 'sensitive' or psychic, whose intuitive sympathy with the plant kingdom spurred him on to produce new hybrid fruit and vegetable forms. He is portrayed as part man/part tree.

This plantsman's body or physical 'trunk' is symbolically rooted in the ground. He is planted into a picture where the colour, echoing nature, moves up from lower earthy tones to lighter greens and blues. The gardener holds a plant in his hand. He himself has been transformed into a hybrid to become a humanised tree of life; a modern Green Man.

Not person as plant or tree, but person as place, fuels the imagination of the metaphysical artist de Chirico. This painter incorporated maps, involving his own travels, into his images. This painter/sculptor is obsessed with how we define ourselves in relation to our environment. Incongruous, puzzling, ultimately fascinating de Chirico's layouts recall Shakespeare's basic premise – 'All the world's a stage'.

De Chirico stages personal confusion and ambiguities may prompt us to examine our own *idées fixes*? What parts are we, and those around us, playing or attempting to play? He creates town squares like chess sets. He presents his own angst over the fact that modern times appear no match for the perfection of the classical past. How many of us are imprisoned by nostalgia? Greek statues, such as the broken remains he saw as a boy, are placed out of context in clinical sets, influenced perhaps by his stay in Germany? Human figures gave way in his work to game pieces and automata, precursors of current obsession with living machinery and books and films exploring the possibility of robots eventually taking over the world. He combines formal sculpture and chess pawns. His cast co-exist, but awkwardly.

We all blend the ideal and the ordinary. This artist provides unnerving images where classical statues metamorphose into armchairs, or the folds of a toga become the draperies covering a chair. These domestic images (of classical couch potatoes) are telling. How many people are welded to their homes, unable to venture out? The blank faces and impersonal bodies of his creations meld person and place. Figures are formed out of architectural salvage. Amalgams of temples and posts, symbols of living archaeology, suggest people becoming ossified. Rousseau's statement that 'man, born free, is everywhere in chains', is echoed in de Chirico's work. Metaphysical angst numbs his figurines in their lifeless sets, no doubt illustrating the key qualities of the painter's own mind; as within so without.

Bo Jeffares Sekine,
Staged Landzscape

It is curious to see how artists adapt their basic beliefs (a personal questions and answers game about reality) by playing with different media. When Bernini, the exuberant, baroque architect, experimented with stage design, he employed shock tactics. If he staged fires or floods fearful theatre audiences leaped up and fled from their seats.

De Chirico also experimented with the theatre. His complex oeuvre spans stage designs, sculpture, painting and illustration. But the same obsessions always resurfaced. Hybrids between man and the environment mixed domestic and landscape features. Weird statues and manikins are set in surreal blends of urban and rustic imagery. People and architecture cross-fertilise. In his theatrical designs, such as those he produced for Diaghilev's dancers in 1929, old themes were continually restated. A dancer's leg, for example, was shown as a pillar. Even tiny details, such as the dancers' socks, patterned like bricks, fit into this all-engrossing fusion of bodies with buildings.

De Chirico's combinations of stately and ludicrous pieces seem oddly convincing. We all have higher and lower selves. We all combine sublime potential with daily limitations – seeds of perfection, feet of clay. De Chirico seems to present incongruous figures as aspects of his own personality (or problems), like so many actors in search of a producer. See his personal choice of titles such as *The Painter's Family* or titles referring to his own bedroom, such as *La Mia Camera* and *Camera Mediterranea*, 1927–8. Perhaps his domestic parables, such as his parody of the epic journey, *Ulysses Returning*, where humans seem partly heroic, partly mundane, sum up a fairly normal, if disconcerting, human polarity.

The next stage, not person as plant or place, but object, is explored by both Magritte and Picasso. The latter, for example, decorates a jug to look like a woman. Comedy, a sure way of making a serious point, is often pure technique. Unexpected juxtapositions or reversed norms can deflate pretension, instigate reappraisal and trigger automatic re-evaluation. Surely this is an essential element in all our evolutionary processes?

Swift, the eighteenth century satirist (and literary inventor of the Yahoo) played with scale to challenge conventions in *Gulliver's Travels* (1726). De Chirico played a similar game. The artist adapted scale in relation to people and their surroundings. His portrayal of the archetypal heroic traveller Ulysses, the brave explorer, questions traditional values. This mythical character has his status subtly undermined by being transplanted into a domestic setting. Europe's number one Super Hero, or the idea of him, is set, or confined, within a modest personal space – the painter's own bedroom.

This personification of the classical past is deliberately placed out of context. The mundane and the marvellous mix as a classical ideal is reviewed within a contemporary time-frame, edited, literally cut down to size, domestically downsized. De Chirico deals with his own obsessions, expressing a fixation with the epic past, a nostalgia perhaps pointing up ideas about his own insignificance? Bedrooms in de Chirico's work can incorporate rocky cliffs and classical façades. They include ambiguous landscape features. A waving line at the side of a rug could be interpreted as a woven pattern or a wave. There is an ambiguous juxtaposition of bourgeois and benign, prosaic and perfect, Greek temples plus comfy chairs. These are the juxtapositions of modern comics and contemporary cartoonists. These are the kind of contrasts which enable us to play games with absurd beliefs and obsessions. We flex mental muscles to make sport of egotistical and suburban selves and thus start to instigate internal change.

Contrasting polarities between positive and negative landscapes, heavens and hells, lush gardens and burnt out wastelands, give traditional reference points. Sometimes the set negativities of early hells, and their repetitive imagery, even if artistically distorted (as in Bosch's contortions) offer no match for intense scenes of private torture.

Goya, for example, suffered tragically and created heartfelt records of his personal fears and nightmares. Recent artists such as the equinox painter Paul Nash, were employed by their governments to capture atrocities during the Second World War. This gifted landscape artist recorded desolate images of No Man's Land, scenery decimated by bombs and carnage. Breaking old conventions, including those in the art world, this ferocious war also helped to smash old barriers to trigger social change symbolised by the public health service.

The painter R.B. Kitaj later drew on *The Wasteland*, T. S. Eliot's discordant poem, to create a deliberately disjointed image *If Not, Not* (1975-6). This includes a strangely-tinted picture featuring the Jewish artist himself within a fractured setting. It symbolically includes the gate of Auschwitz. A strange asymmetrical allegory, dream-like and hauntingly sad, this weird landscape is a complete reversal of Bellini's balanced composition defined by its optimistically welcoming open gate.

Individual complex, personal works cannot be absorbed in a moment. Their ambiguities and mystery touch inner chords. It seems hard to view them, or discuss them, or even to try to recall their essence without recalling feelings, recollecting distant distilled, personal experiences. The other side of the coin – instant recognition – can derive from simple symbol making. A yellow circle for the sun is widely understood. Artists using this kind of aesthetic reduction transform their work – such as abstract codes for environmental features – into universal art. The carefully reduced tree and plant forms gracing Persian carpets and tiles, for example, remain timeless symbols of natural growth.

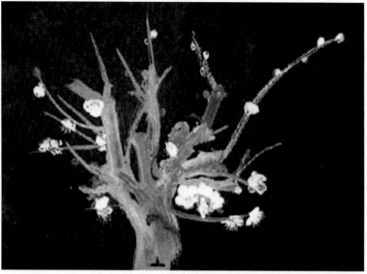

Bo Jeffares Sekine, Blossom

In Japan, plants and flowers can adorn ceremonial costumes. Early plum blossoms or evergreen pines define family crests. Adventurous kimonos can sport whole landscapes. People can literally wear a wave. Designs reveal a subtle range of overlapping techniques involving stylised painted, woven, dyed, embroidered and appliquéd skills. Scenic patterns, featuring rocky outcrops, flowering cherries or autumnal maples decorate a wearer's back or embellish their hemline. Portable pictures include natural and man- made features, rainbow arcs with rustic bridges.

When Noguchi was asked to consider a new, healing landscape for Hiroshima, one of the cities the Americans destroyed with atomic bombs in World War II, the sculptor conceived the idea of double bridges within a Peace Park. He wished to move away from the physical and emotional destruction unleashed by the bomb, trying to focus on positive co-operation expressed by the symbolic hope of building bridges instead of boundaries.

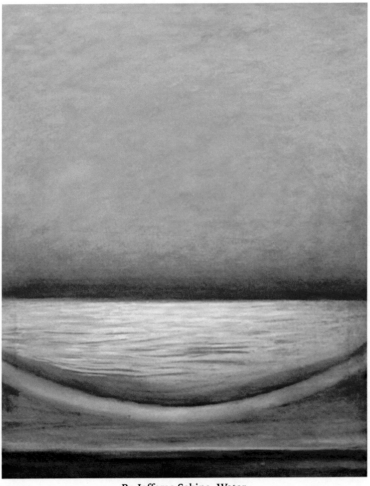

Bo Jeffares Sekine, Water

Waves represent eternal flux charted by modern physics and inspiring kinetic art. Their endless give-and-take is echoed in Ian Hamilton Finlay's concrete poem *Waves*. This poet plays with the concept of 'waves' by adapting lines of visual patterns to suggest wave formations. Thus the word 'waves' becomes a visual metaphor for his expression of ceaseless energy flow.

Invisible energies jump national barriers. Consider how long it would have taken to smooth, mark, parcel deliver a piece of compressed earth, dried bark or papyrus compared with today's instant copying, printing and electronic transmitting. The internet and associated technologies speed up abilities to share information and witness events happening in far off places. Exotic landscape scenes, once an escape route for lone romantics, can now be experienced touristically or appreciated ready-made via the web.

Bo Jeffares Sekine, Noguchi's Heaven, Series

Archetypal images inform our subconscious minds to provide a shared pool of knowledge. Realism remains relative. Defining reality, some people concentrate on their material surroundings, while others like to include more intuitive or creative elements to explain their current definitions of life.

Given that paradise is described by many major religions as a garden, attitudes towards this perfect place monitor our spiritual aspirations. Mediaeval adaptations of paradise tended to be tightly structured, layered, glazed and richly jewel-encrusted. Such images were often enriched with fine details, expressed in expensive pigments. Azure blues created from ground-down lapis lazuli, could cost more than gold. These were treasures, painstakingly produced by the gifted few for the exalted few.

Remember how Bellini opened out the restrictions of the enclosed garden, expanding the viewer's vista, helping to open the way for modern landscape painting? Paul Klee created an unnamed work in Munich which dispenses with any solid worldly boundaries. No land is visible. Any implied action takes place in the air, in space itself. There are no visible actors on stage, so the implication is that this is not a standard religious set piece. There seem to be no established parts, practices or rules of behaviour of the 'knock at the gates of heaven, and St Peter will let you in' variety. This is an ambiguous metaphor.

Has Klee produced a personal invitation, or reference to his own private life, or perhaps both? Nothing is standardised. We have a ramshackle drawing of ladders, lines and levels. Yet this joke, like a drunk tramp or mime artist's fantasy, or flimsy set in an absurd ballet, is provocative. His thin, black, sketchy, surreal scaffolding (worthy of Beckett), provides the antithesis of

Bellini's balanced composition. It is shown off against a clear sky, topped by an indiscriminate blurred mess. This is a deliberately dirty, mucky, cloud above which is a perfect golden globe of a sun. The whole seems an individual allegory for evolution. Klee believed that we must all face hardships, as symbolized by his pollutant cloud. We must deliberately move through hard times and tough challenges, before emerging into lighter situations, seemingly symbolized by his clear, spherical sun.

Moving from two-dimensional art to three-dimensional sculpture, compare the sculptor Isamu Noguchi's three dimensional image – *Tengoku, or Heaven, Water and Stone* sited in Tokyo (1997–8). Noguchi was a 'reductive' master of adult's parks and what he called children's 'playscapes'. A versatile artist, he juggled multimedia, capable of working with metal, paper, clay or stone or the earth herself.

Noguchi worked with wood, canvas and rattan on a theatre design for Martha Graham's *The Embattled Garden* in 1958. Adapting the apple, a constant symbol of pleasure (as in Adam's temptation) he created a set featuring the 'apple on a grand scale'. Its raised platform was coloured like apple skin, with branch-like forms springing out of it and with a tree to the side.

He learnt how dancers moved around his scenery, perhaps also learning valuable lessons about how people interact with sculptural shapes. This may have influenced his later *Heaven* or stone stage in central Tokyo. Here, we are not looking at a mediaeval jewelled enclosure, nor Bellini's open allegory, nor Klee's ladder to light, but a solid, three dimensional place, a contemporary heaven-on-earth. Its theme fits in with pantheist, or Shintoist, views that heaven can exist here and now, basically as an ideal state of mind.

Asked to create a peaceful oasis within a metropolis provided a challenge. Noguchi's brief was to alter a large existent area at the entrance to a modern glass-fronted building specifically built to promote flower arranging demonstrations or *ikebana.*

How did he do it? An existent structure was adapted to become 'more like nature'. Opening up the ceiling let in more light, he made a stone hill and replaced old railings with boulders to create a more open effect. Steps were realigned to meet water flowing down from a high source as in so many Japanese gardens, which he thoughtfully described as 'small stages for the theatre of the world'.

Noguchi's emphasis on clear water descending naturally (rather than being forced up into unnatural fountain shapes) its clarity being contrasted with rough, hard rock belong to the Eastern landscaping tradition. Stone is the essential material in Japanese gardens. And it is significant that he went to the trouble of importing Japanese stone to incorporate into his garden design for the UNESCO headquarters in Paris.

Where Klee contrasted clean with dirty, graphic with blurred, Noguchi showed transparent water trickling gently over metal or rough, natural and polished granite. Rock always equals durability and suggests stability. Water, on the other hand, implies purity and fluidity. His structure is composed of asymmetrical checks and balances. Liquid water, flowing down from a central source to ground level, is balanced by sequences of concrete, anchored steps. Flights of ascending steps like these often symbolise aspiration.

No static heaven, this paradise is deliberately designed to host creative interchange. Envisaged as an arts centre, Noguchi's heavenly 'hill' serves as a teaching site, which has to be adaptable for music or dance or flower arranging extravaganzas. Lorry loads of flowers and foliage arrive to be integrated into his sculptural stage to celebrate seasonal change. This changeability (the essence of *ikebana*) gives Noguchi's stone and water construction life. Also, being a paradise anyone can see and visit it is a fine monument to democracy, suiting an art form which can start with a single flower.

Bo Jeffares Sekine, Detail, Sun and Spiral

This central site is blessed with the rare luxury of living trees. They can be seen on all sides and are reflected in its huge plate glass windows. There is the added rarity of a tree glimpsed through a far window at the back of the stage. The artist has also added a bare, skeletal tree, a pared-down reference to the tree of life perhaps, or a reminder of nature's crucial role in all our lives?

In his *Imaginary Landscapes* Noguchi designed a play mountain for children. He made small, sculptural models for a United Nations' playground. He saw the Earth as one vast shared playground. Feeling he was a citizen of the world he suggested that we should all think globally, reminding us that our combined heritage is now 'the world.'

Mindscapes

Our relationship with the environment is represented by the way in which we choose to see our surroundings. What do we select? What do we ignore? How do we consequently reveal ourselves in relation to the rest of the planet?

Young children's drawings of their homes often show a house with a chimney even if they are living in a flat. They can produce stereotyped, symbolic dwellings, often adding a low green line for earth and a high blue line for sky. They sandwich their view of reality between earth and sky. If happy, they personalise their picture with a huge round, smiley sun.

When they include figures, vital characters such as the artists themselves are often enlarged out of all proportion. Contented children tend to place themselves in the centre of a page, canvas, web design or any symbolic space.

This central focus is equally true for adults. Many draw or describe themselves encircled by their next-of-kin, and/or material obsessions. Marking out these basic ratios provides clues to key factors in each life. Spatial choices clarify identity, relationships and future aims. Seemingly surreal, this kind of image-making (whilst less logically accurate than a photograph) can be much more rewarding, illustrating psychological truths.

Landscape games, where people choose to depict themselves as specific trees, birds, or animals can help to define their world view. Similarly, any choice of marks such as lines, dots, smudges or shapes are valuable if they mean something to their creator.

The simplest doodle can reveal inner feelings or can lead to more expressive experiments. Art provides adaptable tools for emotional visualisations.

Two very opposite but easily assimilated methods of making figures in frames are demonstrated by Leonardo and Turner. Leonardo drew a balanced figure of a man in a combined circle and square; an ordered, geometric symbol. It has mathematical stability. It is logical and linear. It is a visual product of classical Renaissance thought.

Bo Jeffares Sekine, Dissolving Barriers

Turner espoused mystery. He created a deliberately blurred, atmospheric image fusing an ideal entity with space. There is an emotive grace to his angel at the end of a vortex of golden light. It evokes the kind of romantic yearning Baudelaire later defined as 'aspiration towards the infinite'.

Idealism inspired Bellini's *Spiritual Allegory*. He created an imaginary place to evoke the Renaissance dream of spiritual rebirth. He incorporated Christian ethics and classical culture, the latter suggested by the centaur on his shoreline. Optimism colours his work. It is wise and peaceful.

Magritte, on the other hand, frequently demonstrated a negative mindset, portraying how inner limitations can lead to outer restrictions. We continually create prisons and paradises in the mind's eye, forerunners of what we then manifest out in the outer world.

A frivolous surrealist placed a live bird in a cage of bread to await results. Birds soar through the air to symbolise freedom. Magritte created a more profound set of images. Instead of just capturing a bird in a cage, he made an image of a man who literally forms his own prison. This person's trunk is replaced by a bird-cage. Its sides are like ribs. The cage is cloaked so that the man's head and legs appear to be joined. Within this dark interior a dove at an open door suggests possible flight, potential adventures.

Experimenting with birds seemingly about to evade capture, Magritte had himself photographed in the same basic pose, complete with cloak and cage. As well as exploring it pictorially, he adapted his theme in three dimensions. What was he trying to communicate? This would make a provoking cover for a self-help book. It seems like a do-it-yourself kit for psychologists linking people's inner landscapes with their outer actions. The old, restrictive enclosing walls of the *hortus conclusus* have metamorphosed, here, into a more private realm. Caged birds with open doors encapsulate the possibility of personal evolution. All change starts from within. Magritte, ever the cynic, entitled his work *The Heaven*.

Simple Symbols

Minimalism simplifies our universal language. Complex hieroglyphics and ideograms work well enough within their own cultural pockets, as defined by geography and time, but now in the age of the Global Village we need an international code. We want instant symbols. Modern technology is swamped with comic strip imagery, kitsch. Why should art be debased just because science is rushing ahead? Imagine Leonardo at the computer, gracefully integrating art and science.

The process of going abstract, defining and simplifying keys to existence varies with each age and personality. Kandinsky apparently fell in love with abstraction when he accidentally saw one of his own canvases upside down! Miro, deliberately adapting his style, made consistent efforts to simplify and streamline his landscape imagery. He condensed shapes and patterns from farm tools and ploughed earth. Then suddenly one day he just woke up and painted differently – he was producing pure abstracts.

Complex images often have simpler equivalents – often more powerful through reduction. The archetypal roads and stages found in works by artists such as Gozzoli and Bellini have modern equivalents. Old enclosures around the *hortus conclusus* gradually unwind. Thus Christo Jaracheff (of bridge-wrapping fame) decided to stretch twenty-five kilometres of fabric across the Californian desert in 1976. He entitled it *Running Fence*. Richard Long, similarly, laid a set of stones along the floor with the title *Cornish Road*. This places him in the landscape tradition depicting life as a journey. Another conceptual artist, Carl Andre, minimalises allegorical stage sets with a clean cut, classical composition in zinc and magnesium. His floor piece is made up of perfect squares, contrasts of light and dark elements, evoking the game element in life.

Minimalism is rewarding. It boils things down to their essence, drops the dross. Editing refines experience, to create clarity. Fragile flowers can touch our hearts more than piles of gold. Who placed the small wreath of marigolds in the Pharaoh Tutankhamun's tomb amongst his priceless treasures? Similarly, Goldsworthy's petal patterns may stand the test of time in people's hearts when vast stone edifices have lost their power to impress.

Bo Jeffares Sekine, Rainbow Dancer

Specific flowers promote specific concerns. Clean cut lotus and lily shapes, with elegant petals and geometric balance evoke perfection. Such flowers inspire poetic Christian and Buddhist beliefs. Hindus also use lotus shapes in different colours to explain different chakra areas over the body. In contrast, the sturdy, bellicose thistle, known for sharp spikes and barbs, has been selected by tough, traditional fighters, the Scots as an aggressive national symbol. See Mc Dairmid's poem *A Drunk Man Looks At The Thistle*.

Symbolic plants sum up historical eras. The English Tudors' formal double, red and white rose emblem signified tribal peacemaking. Their badge represented the peaceful union of two rival factions, York and Lancaster. The rose, traditionally associated with the Virgin Mary, also gained increased significance when selected as personal emblem by Elizabeth I, a queen politically desirous of virginal status.

Plant types and species can sum up aesthetic movements. Curving, linear convolutions of climbers such as wild roses, honeysuckles and clematis twine their way through the whole Art Nouveau movement whether enhancing Belgian balconies, Irish silverwork or French fabrics. Feminine detail, asymmetric structure and twirling growth sum up these decorative designs.

Renoir, who started off painting roses on china (and would often paint a rose as a warming up exercise before starting a major work) was honoured by having a rose named after him – 'Peintre Renoir'. Some artists become so excited by specific fruits or flowers that they constantly appear throughout their works. Small, natural items create a personal *leitmotif* as with Cézanne's unique apples.

If an artist is obsessed with a specific site, as with Cézanne and Mont St. Victoire, it can be hard to see this subject matter afresh, through unbiased eyes. An artist's vision is often so convincing that their interpretations of nature become hypnotic. Style and content merge. It is like seeing the film before you read the book. Once you have seen a memorable version, you feel aesthetically programmed; visually vaccinated.

Van Gogh's sunflowers bounce out all opposition. His visual recreation of these thick stemmed, sculptural plants with their fat buds, robust flower heads and heavy seed pods is dramatic. Thick paint in ochre, cadmium and chrome is laid on with a rough knife like butter. Flamboyant microcosms of the Mediterranean climate, his versions of sunflowers capture the essence of these miniature sun discs designed to tilt and follow the sun's moving rays.

Like attracts like, as Baudelaire explained in his poem 'correspondences'. Each of us has their own links with nature. Lord Townshend, the eighteenth-century landowner, and well known drainage freak, plus propagator of turnips, was known affectionately as Turnip Townshend. Indeed 'Turnip' is now a registered name issued by the Japanese government in 2004 (along with 'Sardine', 'Beetle' and 'Sparrow') in the official register of legal names. George Wylie, jazz musician and constructionist, made his own subspecies for a public gallery in Glasgow, linking art and music, welding metal trumpets into flowers.

Just as simple flowers appeal directly, so private patches can inspire individual passions. Derek Jarman's idiosyncratic plot sums up personal gardening, as opposed to standardised municipal grandeur. Ironically, he found his site while searching for a suitable bit of woodland to include in a film called *The*

Garden. His adaptive attitude made his garden a lasting tribute to a sick person's ability to continue to create. Before dying from Aids, he and his helpers collected junk from his wind-blown beach beside a nuclear power plant and cherished the toughest weeds. His quirkiness paid off.

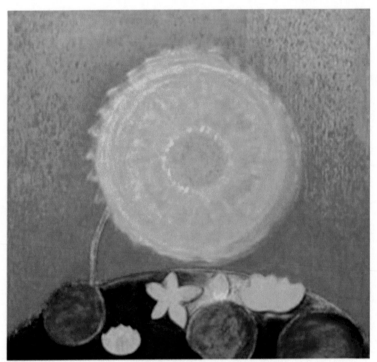

Bo Jeffares Sekine, **Sunflower**

And his love of detail made it unique. All the architectural perfection of a mechanically stylised garden, such as the cubist boat-shaped garden at the Villa de Noailles, can't really compete with such a well-loved, weird and wonderful one. In a book of comments and photographs documenting this little garden's germination and construction, he includes a significant image of himself posing on Monet's wisteria-covered bridge. By placing himself in this long tradition of practical paradise makers, he inspires us all to create our own symbols of perfection, anytime, anywhere.

Just as Jarman proves that a site is secondary to the condition of each individual creator's mind, so Andy Goldsworthy indicates his imaginative capacity to transform the simplest of materials into enticing imagery. Deceptively child-like, he provides a refreshing antidote to technological expertise. Some of his smallest, most minimal works are most memorable. His flower pictures evoke the innocence of John Clare's nature poems, or the freshness of the daily blooms offered to household gods in Bali.

Where Goldsworthy's ready-mades with petals and leaves on rocks or streams dazzle the eye, many of his experiments are tonally restrained. Small circles of flowers are matched by larger rock arenas. Sculptural enclosures derive from stone sheep pens built by adapting dry stone dykes. Some of his materials are easily available, often found, frequently free.

Derided by Long, the long distance walker, as a mere decorative artist Goldsworthy is just as profound in his own, unique way. Trees, branches, sticks and cones are manipulated to provide sensitive, if oblique, comments on nature's basic structures and perennial cycles. His photographic sequences recall nature's endless changes. Tricking time, the artist envisaged and constructed a series of *Midsummer Snowballs* (2000), reminding urbanites of rural life. Made up in the north, over two winters, these were stored, frozen and freighted down to London. In the capital, their dissolution was carefully stage-managed; a deliberate melt down. They were photographed as they slowly dissolved to reveal their inner contents, barbed wire, agricultural tools, feathers – and seeds.

Another deliberate disintegration project, designed to be activated not by heat but water, involved less fuss, less organization and probably less cash flow. This construction, within most people's range, was simple but effective. The full title or description reads:

> stick dome hole
> made next to a turning pool
> a meeting between river and sea
> sticks lifted by the tide
> carried upstream
> turning

The key word here is turning. Goldsworthy's artificial nest of old sticks, sticks in the mind. The drift wood the artist collected, from tiny pieces defining the central space, to increasingly large pieces of wood overlapping this empty circle, was photographed on a river bank. Inevitably, rising tides dislodged and floated his structure away into the evening light. Strategically placed, it turned and turned until it dissipated. Uplifted, moved and rocked by waves, it began to unlock, unfurl and gradually unwind. Slowly and sequentially it unravelled, like a spent coil or gyre, recalling Yeats' archetypal image of breakdown, anticipating the inevitability of change

> Turning and turning in the widening gyre
> The falcon cannot hear the falconer;
> Things fall apart; the centre cannot hold;
> Mere anarchy is loosed upon the world…

copyright © Andy Goldsworthy, Fox Point, Nova Scotia, Canada
10 February 1999

Remember Leonardo's dramatic sketch of a vortex of energy whirling into shape, as he captures the eye of a storm? Basic formations can be as prosaic as water rushing into a drain or matter sucked into a black hole. Here, sticks break loose from a central coil, just as stars are flung out from spiral nebulae in outer space. One of nature's basic mechanisms is demonstrated with a few twigs, as simply as Newton's classic demonstration of gravity with a single falling apple.

How many creative processes stem from self-belief reinforced by visualisation? Tim Smit, creator of the well-named *Eden Project*, is a perfect example of someone who is able to conceive a mental blue-print, and then materialise it. In fact, he says that if he believes in something strongly enough he knows for sure that it will happen. A musical organiser turned gardener, he has channelled his creative abilities into promoting care for the environment.

Peter Randall – Page; Seed Sculpture, Eden Project

Publicising the fragility of our ecosystem, Smit set up micro-climates in geodesic domes. By transforming an industrial wasteland (former Cornish clay pits) he proved himself a practical idealist. The *Eden Project* stresses our reliance on vegetation not just for the air we breathe, but for many other aspects of life including dyes, building materials, industrial components, toys and essential foods.

His choice of the word 'Eden' is ironic. He says he chose it because we 'need to eat more from the tree of knowledge in order to return to paradise'. His Eden popularises eco-friendly designs, sustainable living. It is significant that this *Eden Project's* education centre is symbolically named the Core Centre. It thus shows a symbolic affinity with all nature. Its roof is designed according to the mathematical fibronacci principle, whose expansion ratios (revealed in the structure of daisy heads, sunflowers and pineapples) inspire endless natural formations. At the centre of this building is a reminder of how all plants and projects start. Pride of place was given in 2007 to a stone sculpture again demonstrating the fibronacci pattern – Peter Randall-Page's seventy ton symbolic 'seed'.

Where Smit bottles microclimates, Kew stores seeds. Kew's seed bank is a living library. De Vries, a Dutch botanist turned artist, also attempts to promote natural growth. Carefully enclosing wild land, he created a significant art work, an indication of the changing way in which we are starting to reinterpret our relationship with the earth. Whereas before we felt justified in trying to control nature and impose our own, limited values on her, we now finally begin to sense and appreciate her true value.

Old Paradise gardens were seen as precious, formal enclosures to symbolically protect us from the dangers of the wild. But De Vries reversed this mental pattern. Instead of a cultivated place isolated in a desert or jungle, he enclosed an area of wild land within a cultivated site. He called it a *Sanctuary*, synonymous with a safe haven. In his *Sanctuary* (1997), he made a circular enclosure to protect a small area of self-seeded ground within the confines of a formal municipal park. This is a complete reversal of how we viewed our planet. Now nature is the jewel, man the danger.

De Vries stated that his mission was to 'make visible' that which people no longer saw. He said that he saw his work as a 'social contribution' to general consciousness. Here, in his sanctuary for natural regeneration in Münster, he shows how when nature is left to herself she reforms, or recolonises, on her own terms. His primary aim is to re-educate 'civilised' contemporaries to nature's unique gifts.

His *'Tree Museum'* in The Hague refers to living trees. He went to great trouble to acquaint local residents with each tree's specific qualities and characteristics – combining historical, botanical and social background. By selecting the title *'Tree Museum'* rather than park or landscape garden, he tries to help contemporaries recreate age-old links with trees, relearn their age-old 'relationship' with nature. Urbanites in concrete jungles are re-introduced to a unique blend of scientific fact with respectful pantheism to regain their appreciation for trees. Renewed awareness of the unique qualities of each species contributes to a holistic approach. De Vries listed hundreds of plants and herbs which he had consumed. To reinforce the idea that you are what you eat: he entitled his list: *i am what i am: flora incorporata.*

Similarly, Dr Bach a gifted practitioner of first orthodox and then homeopathic medicine, discovered that specific species cured specific imbalances and their resultant physical symptoms. A tree's structure and growth can give clues to its curative properties. Willow is a fast growing, flexible tree. Its innate elasticity traditionally makes it perfect for fencing and for weaving baskets and lobster pots. Just as willows physically bend in the wind to survive storms, when others break or snap, so its chemical essence can help with emotional flexibility. Medicinally, willow can replace negative tendencies. Its bark provides salicin a key ingredient in the drug aspirin. Dr. Bach used willow as a cure for resentment to stimulate overall vision, to activate a sense of personal responsibility and create an ability to detach and appreciate the comic aspects of life.

Specific trees hold deep-rooted places within our collective consciousness. Olive trees, for example, used by Dr Bach to combat physical exhaustion, were prized by the Greek goddess of wisdom, Athena. Her trees were only destroyed when invaders were intent on long-term punishment for their adversaries because highly-valued olive trees could take generations to mature fully. Olive oil had many uses which included food, cosmetics and lighting. Olive branches also traditionally symbolised peace. More recently, we have chosen olive branches to decorate our United Nations logo.

Leaves and Lungs

Trees have taken millions of years to reach perfection. Although we are relative newcomers within the earth's eco-system, we threaten all the other existing, interwoven species. Everyone tackles this problem in their own way, but sometimes an artist's metaphors about trees of life can be more memorable than a politician's rhetoric about the perils of climate change.

Artists select specific trees for their traditional associations. Bay trees, for example, have long adorned sculptures, paintings and mosaics, being revered for their elegance. Great classical monuments, murals, cameos, coins, pottery and victory wreaths often feature bay leaves. They smell exotic, and they make food taste delicious. The bay, a resilient, perfectly shaped evergreen, is traditionally associated with providing shade throughout the Mediterranean.

The Renaissance painter, Bellini, chose a small bay tree as the central feature of his famous spiritual allegory. A later Italian made a more dramatic statement to remind us all that our existence depends on the health of the world's vegetation. He didn't choose a tidy topiary tree, but a wall of real leaves. In *Respirare L'Ombra / To Breathe Shade* (2000) Giuseppe Penone's evocative combination of massed leaves and human lungs, points up our pollution problems. No trees, no people. No leaves, no lungs.

His lungs are composed of hard metal leaves. They are attached to a large wall or cage of real, organic leaves. The latter dry out loosing colour and fragrance behind their manmade mesh. They provide a vast organic background to a small pair of 'human' lungs. Breathing and photosynthesis go together. Trees and people co-exist. We share the same air, light, water and earth, but we still take trees for granted. This artwork's fresh leaves fade, but its metallic lungs remain cold and still. It is a static image apparently devoid of energy or optimism.

Bo Jeffares Sekine, Leaf Heart

This seems a miserable metaphor. His deliberately mismatched verb and noun, *breathe shade*, provoke contemplation. The artist's line of thought, his reaction to life, appears to evoke nature's bounty and our responsibilities; forfeit one, lose the other.

Green politics inspire international politics and works. Land artists provide a stimulus for global society. Often neither traditional sculptors, nor traditional landscapists, they are frequently trained in other areas such as botany. This new area of influence is shown up by comparisons with earlier landscape painters and more traditional figurative sculptors.

Recalling earlier artists' preoccupation with nature, or – more precisely – their patrons' preoccupation with nature (to fulfil their own desires), we can sense differences between early artists and subsequent creators. The latter follow their own dictates more easily, try to salve their own consciences. Prophets of pollution, they are hopefully free enough to awaken environmental awareness in others.

Earlier, landscape was usually depicted in relation to human activities: it provided a seasonal setting for agricultural or pastoral scenes. Nature could be fashioned into mythical or allegorical modes, as with Botticelli's delicate depiction of the goddess Flora. Links between man and his environment were often symbolised by images of cyclical growth. Images of the seven ages of man were popular. These provided telling comparisons of bouncing lovers in flowery glades contrasted with tragic old wrecks collapsed on withering tree stumps.

Most empty scenes had at least one token figure. A distant fisherman on a lake, or a sad saint in a cave could add an element of human credibility or help to establish a sense of scale. Many later landscapes became synonymous with relaxation. See Watteau, Seurat and Dufy's concoctions of outdoor holidays and festivities. Amorous adventures, formerly enhanced in painted scenes, now proliferate in film sets.

In the past when kings and emperors wanted political domination they demanded huge, flattering, portraits of themselves to adorn territorial pillars and posts. They commissioned massive statues to dominate their subjects. Power trips of ancient and contemporary dictators appear identical. Statues seem to be raised and flattened with monotonous regularity. However as three dimensional artists have gained more freedom to express their own interests, they produce more relaxed, personal and abstracted works.

The sculptor Henry Moore's stylised family groups were placed in his own grounds. Duchamp's 'ready-mades' have their own organic equivalents. The 'arte povera' movement, advocating the use of natural materials (such as Penone's bay leaves) helps new minds mould matter into new concepts.

Acting as agents provocateurs, some of these new land artists become metaphysical catalysts. Compare Bernini's polished marble statue of Daphne metamorphosing into a tree where her delicate fingers turn into leaves and her toes transform into roots, with Penone's *Respirare l'Ombra*. The latter seems crude. But where Bernini's unmatched virtuoso piece gains from a wealth of classical knowledge and professional expertise, Penone's may be quicker to accept, swifter to remind us of vital links between us and nature.

Just as the rainforests are now accepted as the lungs of the world, so our attitude to vegetation is improving. From being background material, or mere cash crops, plants are now being reappraised and nurtured as a vital life source. Native species are being reintroduced. Weeds are being reclassified, appreciated as wild food and wild flowers.

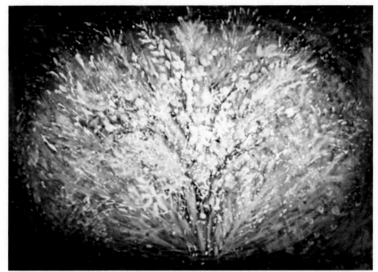

Bo Jeffares Sekine, Growth

There is renewed respect for indigenous woods. There are not only moral, political and aesthetic issues here, but stark ecological priorities. Forest managers set up sculpture trails, commissioning artists to work in woodlands. And world heritage sites are established to try to redress natural imbalances. *Tree Mountain* in Finland has been given government protection for four hundred years, and is described as a 'Living Time Capsule'. The local Finnish Ministry of the Environment and the United Nations Environmental Program combined to sponsor the planting of ten thousand trees by ten thousand people from all over the world as a potent symbol of unity.

In the past, even minimally literate societies used sculpture to record attitudes or create publicity. Masons and carvers often materialised a specific tribe or culture's beliefs. Sacred texts and political claims were 'set in stone'. Triumphal monuments publicised god-like rulers in full regalia. Battle propaganda showed victories over authentically dressed but suitably squashed foreigners. In an age of over communication, modern sculptors (perhaps as a reaction) now prefer simpler means for simpler messages.

Natural materials, artlessly arranged, represent a deliberate move away from ostentatious display. Could this new, self-conscious primitivism provide a counterbalance to growing technological supremacy? Ancient pieces of land art, such as stone and medicine circles, were commissioned or sanctioned by tribal leaders. Constructed for serious reasons, they functioned as astronomical centres, burial sites and focal points for communal ritual.

Self-motivated land artists tend to work for themselves, and often at a tangent to society as a whole. Their combined themes do however overlap and they do illustrate a cultural shift. Their works are not valued in the way jewel encrusted paintings were in the past but are cherished for the ideas which they embody, and the concepts which they seek to communicate.

Walk or Fly?

Long, classified as a conceptual artist, brings us full circle. He reminds us that everything begins with an idea or a feeling. Ideas come first, objects later. This natural progression as minds mould matter is illustrated by many earth artists. Their work is there for us all to see, appreciate, criticise and then adapt in any way whatsoever.

Marks made on the landscape and photographed by Long as part of his circular and cyclical walks provide a case in point. He considers them an art form. This is tantamount to saying that we are all artists, and that the whole of life is a creative game. We are, and it is. Life equates with expression, or at the very least, reaction. Picasso said: 'Art is what I do'. As what we do is dependent on our core-beliefs, it often pays to examine these home-made hopes and limitations. They provide the blueprints for our future. So, watching land artists choosing and formalising their obsessions can be useful, whatever our field of vision, as they illustrate minds at work, and show how ideas inform actions.

Long, in particular, seems to symbolise a free spirit. He is able to travel the world at large. He could be seen as an archetypal wanderer or seer.

For a clear contrast, compare Long's walk to commemorate an eclipse with Gozzoli's Medici commission for an image of the three Magi on a pilgrimage to Bethlehem. This symbolic cavalcade of contemporary bankers adapts spiritual teachings. A contemporary power magnate stars as one of the magi to share in their moral kudos. The early image-maker was a tool in a dextrous publicity department, compared with Long – more of an aesthetic Lone Ranger.

Long self-consciously plans his roads of life. He decides on the theme for his journeys, plots his routes, and then sets off alone. He selects his interactions with nature, decides on the materials he adapts, and those he chooses to record, just as it suits him. Compare Courbet, working a century earlier. This artist was at great pains to foster an image of social respectability. In his self portrait *Bonjour Monsieur Courbet* (1854) the landscape setting is as nothing to the degree of respect with which the artist is greeted, and which he carefully records for posterity. But now landscape and land artists are socially secure, at ease in society, sometimes to the point of being overrated.

Some of Long's earlier works seem scatological. There is, for example, a photograph of his own urine staining the route in *A Walk Across England* (1977) and a memorable shot of a snail, plus its slime, traversing a road. This kind of travelogue featured repetitive images of unremarkable paths, train tracks, canals, gates, signs and so on, very normal scenes which gradually grew to be more visionary.

Deliberately going walkabout in 2001 Chris Drury produced a work entitled *ambulo ergo sum, I walk therefore I am*. Long walked around, placed stones en route (forget motorists) or piled them up into simple shapes. Sometimes he just kicked the ground recording scruffy footprints, stressing the value he placed on his own journeying.

Making or marking *Dusty Boots Line* in the Sahara, in 1988, Long was no different from a child coming home from school, messing about. But he takes his exploits seriously. He studiously photographs effects such as his shadow on the road, a flattened patch left by his sleeping body, or a wet patch where he marked the territory like an aesthetic tom-cat.

He records his effects on the landscape, however ephemeral, as in *Walking a Circle in the Mist*, photographed in Scotland in 1986. This is an image of the temporary tread marks of his footprints on damp, dewy ground. Later trips became increasingly prolific, and included linguistic and topographical records. Site maps (detailing straight and curved meanderings) were marked at set points to record his climatic, geographical and zoological notes. He recorded his personal reactions to heat, cold, wind and sound. Diary entries charted solitary experiences ironically designed, produced and marketed for public consumption. His interactions with the landscape may be displayed in foreign galleries unknown to him, or sold to buyers with whom he has little or no connection. This is a random process. This artist and his audience may be completely disconnected.

Richard Long, A Line in Scotland, 1981

Compare the earth works still created in remote areas like Mongolia by spiritual agents for their communities such as shaman, who preserve traditional belief systems. Their stone lines lead to stone mounds to symbolically preserve a dead person's links with life. A Shaman's stone line curves towards a stone burial mound like a umbilical cord to symbolise a safe return (after a full cycle of existence) to the navel or centre of the earth. These are metaphysical works.

Isolated creativity in Europe was often contrasted with immersion in life experience; ivory towers versus sacred fonts. Now the focus has changed. Long interweaves art and action. Our focus is now on balancing our creative output or personal experience of life with its toll on the planet. We cost up our impact, weighing up future carbon footprints.

Earlier communers with nature, such as Turner, made profitable trips to the Alps and other picturesque places. The artist made prints, watercolours and oils from his observations. Wordsworth, the romantic poet, also manufactured memories. He adjusted sublime scenery. The poet provided an antidote to the Industrial Revolution, just as Long does to our Technological Age. The earth artist once described the hidden or secret aspect of his far-flung sites as an 'antidote to the internet'. Imagine if Wordsworth were alive today. He might set up a very lucrative web site, 'www.lonely as a cloud.com'. For just as the lyricist made a living by distilling his walks around the Lake District, so this creator publishes landscape photographs: updated spin-offs making private journeys public property.

Recalling de Chirico's mental, or memory maps (metaphysical conceits drawing on remembered or imagined journeys) Long's escapades seem naïve. De Chirico, however depressed, introverted, and nostalgic produced work permeated with classical culture. He was a thinking man who drew on a rich vein of Mediterranean references. Long, a later artist, appears less intellectual but is perhaps more expansive. Geographically, jet travel allows artists to travel internationally. Long has visited the Andes and the Himalayas. For suburbanites stuck at home, or packaged into crowded holiday destinations, the freedom of a modern land artist able to explore and experiment in nature's last wildernesses may be breathtaking.

Patterns in Long's mental makeup dictate his life, his working methods and image-making. Blake and Rossetti interrelated visual and verbal imagery. Similarly, Long's memos and jottings complement some of the physical aspects of his achievements. Lists and descriptive phrases could form creative parallels. A compulsive circle-maker, filling and forming circles with slates, sticks and stones, he also concocts typographical circles filled with personal comments.

This conceptual creator enacts physical journeys before recreating them as finished products. He recreates and refines aspects of his experiences, cataloguing his constructs, before commencing new sequences, endlessly moving from action into art. Like all of us, he plans conceives and creates in endless cycles. His plans are so carefully plotted and preserved, that we can become aware, by observing his carefully recorded manoeuvres, of our own evolutionary processes.

Long himself, a man whose main aim is to 'celebrate the world', prefers the work of artists such as Carl Andre. Andre is an ideas man, not someone caught up in the detail of craftsmanship or decorative values for their own sake. Skills and materials are also of secondary value to Long, who feels the best art is always a combination of two factors – the beauty of ideas inspiring physical beauty. Long stresses the fact that we are all linked. We are just one species 'living in the same place in the universe'. No longer just expressing the views of his immediate tribe, like a shaman, he may be more detached from his local community than earlier land artists, but by linking so many different types of global scenery he offers us more of a worldview.

Bo Jeffares Sekine, Snail

Down-to-Earth Inspiration

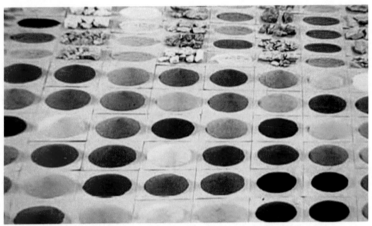

Nikolaus Lang, Detail, Colour Field – Ochre and Sand

Nikolaus Lang is another artist with a universal approach: 'we are only part of the whole.' He created a significant work entitled *Colour Field – Ochre and Sand*. This piece, put together in 1987, links ideas about art, landscape and symbolism. His *Colour Field* is symptomatic of a general urge to explore 'primitive', as opposed to superficial values as when creating images to explore our relationship with the earth. We use the same word both for our planet and for the soil itself.

Lang wanted to re-enact a traditional Aboriginal earth or paint-seeking pilgrimage. Sadly, the tribes who had enacted this ceremonial journey for millennia, had gradually been forced away from their traditional homelands by recent white 'land owners'. Like peoples seeking blessed water from holy wells or sacred springs, or seeking lapis lazuli to paint the Virgin's robes, these nomads had made long treks in gruelling conditions to seek special soil. They then carried this earth over vast distances. No mean feat. This earth, or ochre, was valued for multiple reasons. It could be used to paint bodies for ceremonies, employed medicinally, valued as a gift or blended with fat, water or resin, and to restore ancient tribal paintings or to create new images on bark or stone.

This Aboriginal quest, following the trail of a symbolic emu ancestor, kept their mythology alive. It reinforced links between the land connecting all its species with those who sang its qualities. The deep red soil they collected symbolically represented the blood of their ancestors. How ironic that a European tried to re-enact their ritual journey for natural colours. Aboriginal Australians are now plied with bought paints, chemically calculated pigments, 'perfect' products, plus the whole paraphernalia of western art including standardised, hard-edged, geometric canvases. They can easily forget or neglect their own natural resources, colours they walked across and wore transforming their bodies into artworks.

Colour Field – Ochre and Sand is made from soil samples. It comprises a hundred and forty-four samples of earth in lump form or ground into powder, plus two hundred and eighty-eight sand samples. From the darkest to the lightest, the brightest to the subtlest, there is a vast range of colours. This authentic palette includes pale, warm, subtle, deep browns, blacks, rusts, reds, oranges, apricots, pinks, peaches, creams, yellows, greens, greys and whites. These colour samples spread out – 504 x 600 x 6 cm – to make a symbolic colour field. The whole of Australia is one vast colour field. So is the entire earth.

Another artist with similar fixations, Herman de Vries, also collected earth, ash and charcoal, including samples from Auschwitz. The fact that such a range of artists began to show an interest in the soil itself in its natural state (not as ready-made tubes officially labelled 'burnt sienna' or 'burnt umber') indicates a symbolic change of heart.

There may be a parallel with the way scientists are moving away from concepts of the universe as an impersonal machine and taking a renewed interest in the Greek idea of the earth as Gaia, more of a self-regulating goddess. Mother Earth long plundered and exploited now comes into clearer focus and begins to be re-valued as a living entity. And earth itself becomes valued as a creative ingredient. Significantly when the Eden Project was created, soil from the actual building site was compressed into vast blocks to be formally incorporated into its main entrance. Earth comes into its own again as a creative material, just as the Earth herself regains respect.

There are shifting attitudes towards 'primitivism'. Some painters like Douanier Rousseau are primitives because they may not wish or be able to be anything else. Some, like Picasso, consciously studied 'simple' iconography to incorporate different methods when commentating on life. Like a fusion chef, he experimented with assorted styles and ingredients to create exciting new visual menus.

Picasso's predatory trips to the Louvre to study African masks resulted in Cubism, a new two-dimensional format for presenting three dimensional facts. Similarly, Klee's reaction to academic stultification resulted in fresh change, a new cycle of innocent, child-like art. Compared with these earlier artists, Lang's work can seem strange, macabre, crudely strung together.

See his comment on the destruction caused by human transport, collections of shocking, scarlet, mummified animals, road kill. This artist's symbol-making reveals anthropological objectives. He stimulates environmental awareness, to indicate how our roads of life decimate those of other species.

Early settlers in Australia saw this ancient continent through imported Western eyes. Blinkered by a European mindset, they imposed a mental strait-jacket on all its inhabitants and vistas. Aesthetically pre-conditioned, they 'saw' this alien landscape as an incongruous exploitation site. They were scared and limited, trying to impose their own cultural patterns on alien spaces, fauna and flora. Aborigines were largely seen as picturesque or sub-human. 'Savages' populated an unnatural place, full of peculiar plants and weird animals. Such oddities were neither valued in their own right, nor treated on their own terms. There is a vast difference between early colonial imagery, nostalgic attempts to recreate remembered rose gardens, with later more authentic 'views' of this unique continent.

Compare early romanticised sketches with the later semi-abstract landscapes by the Australian artist Sidney Nolan. Nolan's images drew appreciatively on actual aspects of a place with little rainfall, sparse foliage and massive skies. Australia's burnt out natural palette, and blue-grey trees cannot compete with its intense sky colour (as in wetter and greener Europe) so this blue ceiling seems immense, polarising rusty red soils below.

Nolan and his ilk began to see this scenery afresh (just as gardeners began to boast of planting 'native species' which they formerly dismissed as 'scrub'). Nolan tried to express elements of Australia's own landscape mythology. He painted the adventures of Ned Kelly, the outlaw in the saucepan hat, and tried to evoke the Aboriginal Rainbow Serpent. But Nolan's works, however subtly evocative of Australian space, remain within the European pictorial tradition. He used a rubber squeegee, a bit of draught excluder, to get his blended effects, but he painted regular, rectangular pictures for regular, rectangular walls. Would this man have climbed into a crevice to make art?

Lang did. This rather spontaneous experimenter (who originally trained as a sculptor and wood carver) invented his own mental and physical responses as he went along. Discovering an isolated cult site in the Flinders Ranges, Lang was fascinated by this enclosed space, and by its symbolic and sculptural elements. This small open-ended passage was marked with circles, points and spirals with what seemed to be sun signs at each end. Aboriginal artists had smoothed the stone of its walls and floor, and added engravings of native animals such as turtles, geckos, owls and lizards plus animal paws and human hands. Lang copied and adapted these hand prints within his own work, and captured his own footprints in clay.

Why had these images which could not be seen but only felt been created in the first place? Why did people then crawl into this space to intuitively feel them? What did they then experience? Lang's obsession led him to record these images in reverse, like an archaeologist trying to preserve cultural records. He made a three-dimensional cast of the inside of this strange art work, exhibiting it under the title *Brain Ship* (1987-90). Like a modern framer protecting an ancient painting, he had made a modern cocoon to encapsulate a mysterious place.

Practically speaking this was a challenge. His flimsy structure was the result of a week in the heat, compressed into a confined space, pressing paper pulp (made from cotton fibres and rain water) onto its rocky sides. Fine casts produced delicate impressions of its inner structure. He showed these in reverse (like reversing a photographic negative) reinforcing his flimsy panels with sticks, fitted together in his studio. *Brain Ship* commemorates earlier minds making art, but could initiate contemporary people into new awareness. It acts as a creative catalyst inspiring imaginative journeys.

Interconnected Aboriginal beliefs link every aspect of their culture and environment. Richard Long is another example of an artist inspired by this helpfully unified attitude to life. He praises the parallel 'primitivism' and spirituality in the Navaho Indians renowned for their sand paintings. Bruce Chatwin, a writer with similar interests, charted similar territory. He used his skills to record appreciative anthropological curiosity and care. In *Song Lines* (1987), Chatwin described how some Aborigines, being taken for a drive in a truck, suddenly broke into song helpfully 'singing up' the landscape to make it appear, to make it real.

These make an invisible, sequentially linked network which stretches across and connects their whole continent. Songs, part poem, part route march, relive their ancestors' creative interactions with the land. Geographical features are celebrated with stories and mythic events marking out sequences of meeting places and water holes so essential for survival.

Line and country can be synonymous in tribal languages. Safe lines or 'ways out' are vital in a drought-ridden place. The constant tune of a particular route can enable a traveller to move safely from one side of this vast continent to another – moving from mythical site to mythical site – all within one vast, creatively connected territory. Their approach creates veneration for their land. Aborigines singing their song lines consider themselves as co-creators of their environment. Landscape exists in the mind and is materialised through their creative process by 'singing' it into being. In the beginning was the word.

Richard Long, African Footprints

Dream Time, a mythical era of ancestral creation, is alive and well. Flexible as dreams, this spirited realm exists in the continuous present. The present is all that counts. In this, 'primitives' are often intuitively closer to understanding quantum physics than so-called 'civilised' societies. They instinctively appreciate links between life forms and know that matter and energy are interchangeable. It seems symbolic that in their minds they make the landscape 'real' by singing it into being. Matter can equal waves or vibrations. Think comparatively of the symphony of sound waves suggested by the Western concept of the Harmony of the Spheres.

A massive rock like Uluru is a power centre. As well as being a physical landmark it is a sacred site. This immense stone has its own integral energies like the ley lines which emanate from it. These can still be sensed, or psychically felt, by many native Australians who do not all need a dowser's rods, pendulums, or complicated machinery to take electro-magnetic readings of the Earth's invisible power lines and their connection points.

Bo Jeffares Sekine, Triangle

Grounds of Understanding

Energy, when defined in new symbolic forms, is inspirational. New symbols inform *The Garden of Cosmic Speculation*. Changing concepts of existence have long been encapsulated in earth art. In this unique garden abstract ideas 'took shape' amongst trees and vegetables. It was inspired by understanding and explaining evolution. Charles Jencks and Maggie Keswick adapted contemporary scientific breakthroughs in microcosmic and universal fields. Their thirst for knowledge, for pushing the boundaries and definitions of reality, made their garden an entrancing surprise intellectually and visually. Its implied remit was optimistic curiosity, investigating a 'new world' view. Outward looking, inventive, it focuses attention on the future.

Charles Jenks and Maggie Keswick, Garden of Cosmic Speculation

Charles and Maggie, a marriage of true minds, complemented each other's insights and practical abilities. Maggie understood Eastern aesthetic principles. Her childhood had been spent in Shanghai. She adapted *Feng Shui* – the idealised landscape grid created by the Chinese for enhancing spatial possibilities. She had enjoyed and studied Chinese landscaping at first hand. Charles' training in Western architecture, her intuition, his love of modernism and allegory plus her gardening skills, all combined in 1988 to start to create a living work of art.

Maggie inspired a private garden harmonising personal and theoretical concerns. Domestic needs and scientific theories coexist. And after her death, Maggie's memory is kept alive not just by her healing centres for cancer victims, but also by an area where nature is left to regenerate in a garden designed to evolve as it matures.

Working from a family garden shaped by her parents in the Scottish borders, Maggie and her husband tried to fit in with its *genus loci* to appreciate the overall spirit of the place. They tried to sense spatial tensions between high and low areas, and understand the essence of the land and rolling hills about them. Like Barbara Hepworth, making rounded forms with taut strings to suggest the invisible links and connections between geographical features, they tried to respect feelings generated by the natural environment.

They drew on shared features from Eastern and Western cultures, scent and colour, taste and texture, peace and calm. But where traditional sensual and philosophic values such as pleasure and detachment were cultivated, so too were innovation and novelty.

Shock is essential for any understanding of quantum physics, or quantum 'weirdness'. If you are not shocked, you have not started to grasp the apparent contradictions of a system based on strangeness. It seems significant, on reading Jencks' account of how they created their garden, that they consulted 'scientists, gardeners and craftsmen' in that order.

His scientific curiosity led to an open-minded approach. His head gardener, Alistair Clark, had the patience to absorb and understand contemporary science, transforming it into cultivated vegetation. This is reflected in a wide range of stylistic interpretations of scientific theory. Their Garden of Cosmic Speculation includes baroque elements, expressing shock and surprise, surreal features, allegorical conceits, and several pieces of classical perfection.

This is a garden of the mind where virtual reality becomes physically tangible. See how they adapted their old, walled kitchen garden. This enclosed area with its traditional rectangular divisions, designed for raising food for survival, was built to protect plants. But as its owners thought about adapting it, considering first a new Psychic Garden, then a Garden of the Senses, and then a Garden of Common Sense, they became increasingly adventurous. They began to consider ways of revealing common links between us and other weeds and pests. This was to be a vegetable plot with a difference. It was laid out with DNA curves and giant free-standing helix shapes. This multi-layered metaphor, a garden of six senses, illustrates Jencks's desire to translate scientific abstractions and philosophic insights into concrete form.

Jencks stages his own obsessions by metamorphosing science into art. He bends and curves a traditional flat grid (similar to the geometric floor design in Bellini's *Sacred Allegory*) to form a concave curve. Consulting computer graphics he breaks regular forms into fragments to create a *Fractal Terrace*.

Just as Jencks draws on mathematical theory to inform his visual pattern, so he draws on astronomical advances to design a *Black Hole Terrace*. Here another geometric formation is twisted and spun, stretched and warped, into new curvatious forms. His elegant, elastic whirl, blending into a round disc illustrates space/time curves. It is perfect for non-scientists (like me) unable to fathom Einstein's formulae but still wanting clues to vital scientific mysteries.

Jencks is an optimist for whom all negatives are potential positives. A black hole may spawn new energies, universes and realities. Nature is appreciated as self-regulatory, self-healing. Within this overall optimism, contrasts add richness. Reality has always been expressed through opposites such as day versus night, living versus dying, heaven versus hell, love versus hate. Traditional dark and light contrasts, such as the traditional black and white of chess sets so often inspiring artists' stage designs, are replaced in this innovative garden by matt green astroturf set off by silvery aluminium.

Aluminium is also used to create light, free-standing sculptural pieces – whether an atom or a solar system. Those inspired by DNA are equally beautiful in summer sun or with winter snow. These are pure abstracts. Those with the more mannerist additions, which have to be explained to be understood, may not stand the test of time so well. (Similarly, squiggles on his greenhouse roof, scientific formulae decipherable only to those trained in their calligraphic significance, might bemuse some future civilisations.) However the double helixes spiralling through his garden represent ageless geometry, natural, aesthetic symbols of evolution.

If DNA represents part of the cosmic code, essential patterns in life, so too do wave formations. Jencks makes light work with waves. He adapts them in innovatory fashions. His most significant adaptation, within the landscape field, is his selection of a wave form to inspire his boundaries. Traditionally paradise gardens were solidly walled in to sequester them and protect them from the elements, as in his own, old kitchen garden. But this speculative garden or symbolic landscape is mentally and physically designed to interact with the whole cosmos. Instead of a priceless jewel set in a firm enclosure, he produced an evolving site surrounded by a soliton wave. A soliton wave is one which allows others to pass through it, thus symbolising freedom on many levels.

The continuous lines of his asymmetrical fences, integrated walls and asymmetrical plantings interact with each other around his boundaries. This architect is open to new ideas. Jenks designed a site permeable to new possibilities. His fences and gates reflect this open-minded attitude. He often rejects solid impenetrable structures for linear designs in thin, metal strips permitting viewers to look right through into other areas. Many of his wave designs are based on pure science to symbolically link our earth with outer space.

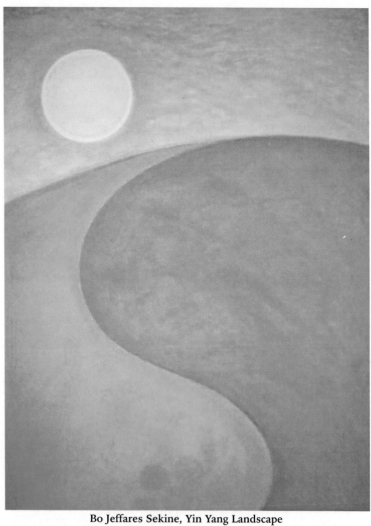

Bo Jeffares Sekine, Yin Yang Landscape

Ideas as Images

Jencks makes us think. Playing with wave forms he reinforces the fact that waves are not just earthly forces. Waves move throughout the universe, a composite sea of waves, composed of endless fluctuations. Did waves exist prior to matter?

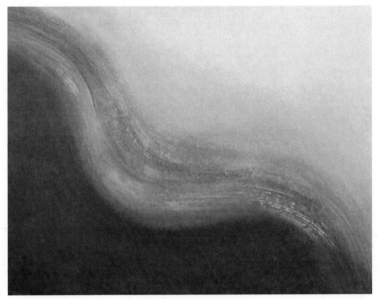

Bo Jeffares Sekine, Wave

Varied energy created by our own bodies, such as our pulses, brainwaves and voice patterns all interlink. Life consists of matter or vibration. Vibrations or waves form invisible landscapes recognised in microcosm within our bodies, and in macrocosm within multiple external universes. Electromagnetic currents align our brains and the earth's ley lines with the energies in outer space. These interactive wave-forms (including our own songs and the magnetic hum of the earth herself) form a membrane of vibrations. This is a single energy web, not a machine but more of an eternal living consciousness.

Chris Drury, another land artist, made a parallel between wind, water and mind all of which are ideal vehicles for wave energy. Thought is now recognised by quantum physicists as a quantum effect – a key factor in any experiment. Each person's input influences each outcome. Like the idea of a butterfly flapping its wings to change weather patterns, or a fragmentary shift in a kaleidoscope altering a whole pattern, each scientist's 'objective' experiment will subtly vary, as different minds mould matter differently, by charging it with their own unique energies.

Artists and architects adjusting our thoughts about existence occupy shifting roles. The boundaries between the projects they plan and produce are equally flexible. Thus, to recap, European landscape painters once rock bottom on the academic scale have become increasingly popular. Monet, for example, once derided as a *plein air* painter has become an easy norm for public taste and perception. One of the first to diversify, Monet moved seamlessly into practical landscaping. Cultivating his lily ponds as light reflectors, he created a natural muse to inspire pictures gracing galleries worldwide.

For Monet, a private paradise inspired personal image-making and helped to bring public recognition. Noguchi, the internationally renowned sculptor and pioneer of earth art, had a garden gallery specifically designed to show off his three dimensional works. Jencks, the architectural landscaper, received a commission from the Scottish Gallery of Modern Art to provide a chance to place his private experiments within the public domain. Linking art and science, as in the Renaissance, he adapted land forms to create personal versions of cosmological iconography, thus creating his own symbols for evolution.

Jencks' imagination was caught by the way in which Nature appears to fluctuate between perfection and chaos, the extremes of Platonic perfection and quantum weirdness. His own projects range from timeless elegance (as with the helix sculptures) to broken form, as with *Fractal Terrace*. Nature, like people, breaks down into sensitive chaos to allow obsolete patterns to dissolve and allow new structures to emerge. Jencks refers to this dichotomy as a polarity between Culture and Nature.

Olafur Eliasson, a Scandinavian with a Nordic craving for the Sun is also curious about how we react to natural phenomena. Eliasson was commissioned by Tate Modern to create work in their Turbine Hall. This building had originally supplied energy, in a practical sense. Now it generates art for the imagination. Eliasson wanted to activate people's feelings, to draw on their experience of the natural world. He was inspired not by facts, but 'the idea' of landscape. So he questioned everyone he came across, chatted with taxi drivers and questioned gallery staff, discovering at first-hand how the British love to reflect on their mood-changing weather conditions. His research paid off. His simulated sun magnetised people, drawing in frozen wintry crowds.

British poets and painters are endlessly inspired by the variable richness of their native landscape. Constable and Turner are renowned creators in this field, adapting facts as starting points for pictorial evocations of intangible effects. Constable's cloud sketches can be realistically checked against meteorological records. Turner's romantic confections prove his desire to 'paint atmosphere', to capture the essence of ephemeral effects such as the sun's luminous rays dissolving fog or mist.

Bo Jeffares Sekine, Solar Power

What would these two earlier, two dimensional landscapists have made of Eliasson's ability to conjure up heat and mist? Manufactured clouds of vapour drifted up towards a mirrored sun. Businessmen, tourists, shoppers and students entered this vast, dusky hall, lit by orange light from a technically created 'sun'. Escaping from cold, outside conditions, many lay down contentedly on the floor, like so many happy insects, staring up at this artificial heat and light source to relax in the warm glow of a symbolic sun.

Before this popular *Weather Project* (for the Tate, in 2003) Eliasson had created *Your Sun Machine*, in 1997. He wished to awaken people to holistic interactions. All his viewers, observing the slow passage of a beam of sunlight from a hole in the ceiling, were themselves an intrinsic part of his tribute to this sunlight. Sunlight brightens our atmosphere physically. It also lightens our emotional moods to make us feel altogether 'sunnier'. Similarly we describe people as 'live wires' whose presence can 'light up a room' or 'generate' optimism. Peoples' reactions make them inclusive parts of the experiment. We are not just passive viewers. We are contributing co-creators. We are an intrinsic part of any creative process.

Continuous connections between us and All-That-Is are literally brought down-to-earth when we use safe, well known elements from our earthly existence, such as fields, to explain more ambiguous or unusual matters. Dr Rupert Sheldrake, an open-minded biologist, wished to sum up the way in which information is mysteriously passed between members of the same species, when they are completely isolated from each other with no physical means of communication. If monkeys on one island, for example, learned a new way of obtaining food, similar monkeys on a different island seemed to immediately share the same knowledge. This morphogenetic synchronicity, where species morph into instant understanding is called the 'M field'.

This succinct phrase ties new knowledge into a traditional symbol. Well known, after generations of practical toiling for food, the field symbol spawns countless derivations. Known in Ancient Egyptian and Chinese ideograms to symbolise man's cultivation of the earth, fields are adapted by varied elements of society to anchor or cement new concepts.

Bo Jeffares Sekine, Balanced Life

Bo Jeffares Sekine, Corn Field

Fields traditionally represent positive interactions with the earth. Agnes Dene reminds us of this fertile imagery, of the need to use the land to grow food. She plants grain in urban sites to shock people into remembering what is essential for survival. She grew food fields in New York and London. Her wheat field on an old industrial site in East London, planted in 2009, came complete with its own outdoor oven for cooking and eating food.

Field imagery can be used to ground abstract thoughts or explain theoretical principles. Physicists, for example, searching for the meaning of life throughout the universe sought a 'Unified Field Theory'. Fields can be used to explain all existence, whether in microcosm or in macrocosm. Thus martial artists teach their practitioners to become aware of their own inner core of psychic or spiritual energy. And they tellingly describe this source of personal power as their 'inner field'.

Computer programmers create 'compulsory fields' to gather data. Our minds move from solid farmers' fields, to metaphysical fields of action, fields of information, fields of knowledge, fields of understanding, fields of consciousness and hopefully fields of merit.

Earth imagery remains flexible. We adapt her symbols to express hopes and dreams.

What landscape symbols would you select to explain your inner mindscape?

How do you envisage your Road of Life, or evolution?

Being Human Catalysts

Space is a constant factor in all our definitions of what it means to be human because space implies relativity. Just as there seem to be solid and more intangible aspects to our own bodies, so there are solid and invisible aspects to all life. We physically convert solids and liquids into energy. Our hearts and minds turn everyday matters, with phrases such as 'hearts of gold', into symbolic terms. Scientists focus on logic to explain the behaviour of the microcosmic cells within our bodies or macrocosmic galaxies interacting in outer space. Artists harness intuition to express emotional and psychic energies. Wisdom combines logic and intuition simultaneously accessing both sides of the brain.

Thoughts and feelings, endlessly repeated, crystallise into beliefs just as stalactites and stalagmites build into architectural form. Similarly, the repetition of prayers and mantras prescribed by religious leaders, healers and various sporting and life coaches develops new thought-patterns. It is not what we want but what we unconsciously expect which arrives from the divine answering service. By changing inner expectations, invisible order forms are altered, subconsciously magnetising different circumstances to create miracles.

Gifts of 'in-tuition' materialise as we concentrate, trust, fully expect and so start to manifest inner truths in outer arenas. 'I have a dream.' Images help to popularise beliefs. The arts provide working tools. 'Real' and 'Surreal' pictures, sculptures, buildings, gardens, films and photographs illustrate how seemingly ordinary materials can easily be transformed. Look at Magritte's leaf trees, or Penone's leaf lungs. Change is the norm. We use symbols to define what currently appears to be 'true'. Space provides a matrix in which we express ourselves.

Bo Jeffares Sekine, Still Life? Seed Explosion / Café

What is your personal 'view point'? Creative minds highlight new points of view to enhance existing spaces or project new perspectives. The way we choose to interpret space sums up our evolutionary stance. Ideally, down-to-earth and visionary components fuse. We are logical. We construct set sites from mathematically measured plans and exactly scaled blue-prints. We are intuitive. We weave poetic imagery in cosmic contexts. We blend abstract and concrete truths, seen and unseen realities. We paint pictures and write plays. Animals don't make symbols. We do. Whether inventing games within 'cyber' space or building playgrounds within 'real' space, we in-form and trans-form the spaces we envisage and span.

Metaphysics allows us to translate the energies of one realm into another whether classed as scientific or spiritual. Solid, three dimensional 'reality' can dissolve – under careful scientific scrutiny – into myriads of particles some of which, ironically, can be in two places at once. Strange discoveries about the ebb and flow of our energetic components make us seem slightly less dense than we had thought. Are we less mud and more music?

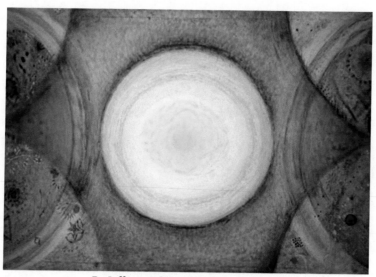

Bo Jeffares Sekine, Rainbow Universe

Members of the medical profession wire us up to study how meditation or molestation affects our electromagnetic systems, stimulating brainwaves, changing heart rhythms. Our pulses are given out regardless of whether we are awake or unconscious. We broadcast our state of mind through the ether as efficiently as our technology communicates its invisible impulses. Radio masts, television towers, computer networks, telephone messages, satellite signals, and human emotions add into a shared matrix. Could becoming more aware of pet hates and deliberately transforming them into flexible optimism make personal broadcasts more caring?

Our creative frequencies, thoughts and feelings, make us unique creative catalysts. But what are we – part of God's dream, or co-creators within an eternal energy field?

Space

Heaven and Hell are the metaphysical spaces where we envisage ideals or project fears. They are given imaginative credibility by successive civilisations. The existence of these archetypal symbols for good and evil, whether seen as imaginary sites, states of mind, or spiritual truths can enrich our moral and cultural choices.

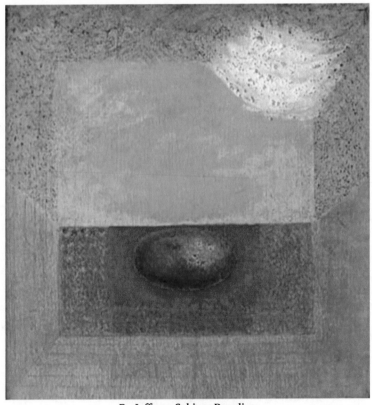

Bo Jeffares Sekine, Paradise

Heaven and Hell, internal states, are defined by physical opposites. Heaven is a temperate, welcoming environment. Heaven allows for freedom and mental expansion. Its space is unbounded. But in Hell it is hard to get a 'Room with a View'. It is synonymous with incarceration, and either too hot or too cold. Its spaces are restricted. You are bottled up, boxed in, mentally and physically deprived of liberty, of spatial freedom.

Where heavenly spaces are envisaged as bright, joyous and welcoming, hellish spaces are dark and depressing. Visions of Heaven enhance earthly experiences, and love is expressed with light and colour. We picture glowing scenes, often placing them inspirationally high above the clouds or way beyond the stars. Hated hell holes (whether domestic or institutionalised) are more tortuously sited within the bowels of the earth, or in more up-to-date versions, within the confines of black holes.

Less fearful, but always boring, are our neutral images of Purgatory, the spiritual in-between stage summed up in war as 'No man's land', or in ordinary life as international airports. All the impersonal bureaucracy of Kafka, all the uniform grey concrete car parks (used for shoot-outs in B films) belong to this dull category. Where purgatory remains bland, Paradise is excitingly exotic. Most religions picture paradise as an exotic environment, a beautiful landscape.

Repackaged by astute travel agents, selling sun, sex and space in tropical locations, Paradise has become an increasingly sensual commodity. Modern paradises are parodied by David Lodge in *Paradise News* (1991), an ironic take on popularised perfection.

Paradise, once an unattainable dream, situated in an unknown venue is slowly coming down-to-earth. Concentration on the

Bo Jeffares Sekine, Infinity Pool: Birds, Cats and Fishes

present, the power point of reality (as advocated by all yoga and meditation gurus) makes the mystical appear a more acceptable part of our existence. Philip Pullman's fiction popularises the idea of invisible 'portals', or doors which can be found, or cut, through time and space to different existences. Scientists are similarly intrigued by ideas of space containing multiple universes, all perhaps co-existing on varied wavelengths?

We can fly through our sky, or beyond it, into areas once mentally set aside for floating spiritual havens. Heaven, heavenly and the heavens are closely related words which reveal their linguistic and theoretical similarities. We associate ideas about heaven, the perfect place, with the heavens, the outer reaches of our spatial comprehension.

In the past, figures occupying the skies tended to be divinities or angels. More recently spiritual democracy has set in with practical pilots, adventurous spacemen and imaginative travellers. Look at the popularity of Chagall's lovers, floating blissfully above the roof tops, their mutual passion releasing them from gravitational and spatial restraints. Surely mental states built on love inspire us all?

How do we make dreams come true? What we feed into our brains, our software, pre-determines resultant 'realities'. Dominant desires and beliefs fuel our futures. By becoming more aware of our metaphysical capacity, consciously focusing our minds, and selecting the words and phrases we program ourselves with, we may have a stronger chance of expecting and materialising positive hopes as individual longings for paradise metamorphose into shared practical visions.

Bo Jeffares Sekine, Building

Building Space

Bo Jeffares Sekine, Town Planning

Building spaces involve imaginative and practical abilities. Buildings traditionally link heaven and earth. In Mongolian tents, for example, the central smoke hole is open to the sky and is called the 'eye of heaven'. Tent owners appreciate their homes as the centre of their private universe. Their tents thus provide a symbolic link between domestic and universal space. We always try to link what we already know with what we seek to explore. So we associate body parts with our constructions. Farseeing eyes, for example, protectively adorn Viking ships and Tibetan temples.

Sexual elements are traditionally attributed to different parts of our buildings. In Mongolian tents, for example, the earth floor and soft, round, fabric exterior are seen as 'feminine'. But the roof structure and square hearth are described as 'masculine'. There is a complementary balance between these male and female elements, just as there is between its living and ancestral inhabitants.

In the wild, we often interpret outdoor spaces in body terms. We like to see particular shapes as echoes of our own bodies. Our earth's curves, caves and crevices, for example, are often equated with the curvature of female bodies, and many rounded hills are connected with mammary processes. Mountains, such as the Paps

Bo Jeffares Sekine, Playground

of Jura, or sites in the Wild West reflect similar obsessions: Bill Bryson in *Made in America* (1994) thought that loneliness had resulted in more 'Nipple Mountains, Tit Buttes and the like than you could shake a stick at.'

Manmade structures elucidate the human condition. Reliable people are praised as 'towers of strength'. Similarly, 'key-hole' surgery explains minute, medical procedures taking place deep within our body tissues. This small but crucial entry point to a building is neatly adapted to explain the minute but vital entrance point for such operations.

We focus on the inspirational 'light at the end of the tunnel'. More abstract, less architecturally defined, is the emotional relief we feel after metaphysically 'pulling ourselves together'. We try to 'rise above' trivial issues. We 'look within' for wisdom. We rejoice when a metaphysical 'weight is lifted off our shoulders', or more importantly 'off our minds'. We attempt to get to the metaphysical 'heart of the matter'. Everyday speech blends body language with abstract geometry as spatial images suggest states of mind. We aggressively 'overstep the mark' or submissively 'toe the line.' We 'draw a line' under events to clarify detachment and thus evoke emotional 'closure'.

Constructing public spaces, people display national characteristics. The Chinese, for example, adapted a bird's nest, one of their most cherished safety symbols, as a focal point for their Olympic arena. How we arrange our toys, solid or virtual, matches our inner cares with our outer obsessions.

'Reality' television shows select specific interiors inviting us to play detective and decide whose house is on view. Collections, decorative decisions, symbolic spacing, natural and technological

110 | *Creativity Nature and Us*

interests all add up. They illustrate how we weave different creative strands of life together. Mental attitudes mark material choices. We are like bower birds. They decorate their mating bowers with colourful flowers, fruit and oddments to attract appreciative mates. People who create dream homes, deciding how to blend into or defy their surroundings, express themselves still further. They have the chance to consider essentials, such as energy supplies, whilst materialising their own private ideals.

Communal Space

We create communal spaces to illustrate group aims and ambitions. Parks provide halfway houses between private exterior spaces such as patios and yards and the countryside at large. Once paradise gardens were depicted as safe enclosures protected from predators. Now the reverse is true. Instead of a tidy geometric space, as perfectly patterned as a Persian carpet, we create 'wild' spaces as an antidote to stressful town lives. We even indulge in 'model farms' (like Marie Antoinette) so that children – once slaves to agrarian duties – can glimpse where food comes from. Historical norms are reversed. Having decimated vital rainforests, and concreted over vast areas of wilderness, we now increasingly seek the reassuring illusion of 'natural planting.'

Bo Jeffares Sekine, Green Park

Central Park is a case in point. New York's organised city fathers, working their grid-like way up Manhattan Island, deliberately selected a 'wild' design for their green centre, their largest urban space. They planned this democratic answer to paradise as a 'natural' site. Subtle, low cut, serpentine cross sections, feature meandering walks, rough rocky outcrops, and bosky trees. This park, which includes a life-sized chess set as well as a_ statue of the young heroes in Frances Hodgson Burnett's classic tale for children, *The Secret Garden*, written in 1911, praising the restorative powers of nature.

Bo Jeffares Sekine, Central Park

Dark rampant undergrowth, plus the threat of fierce creatures lurking in it, terrified our ancestors. Fear made for fences, psychologically blocking out frightening forests and untameable jungles. Now the situation is reversed. We equate larger horizons and unrestricted areas with independence. We feel we need space both physically and emotionally. Space is equated with inner and outer freedom.

In the past, individual trees were often highly respected. Native Americans, for example, would ask the spirit of a tree to share its knowledge, before carving a mask from its body, its living tissue. There was a pantheistic symbiosis between people, as learners, and the elemental forces of nature, as represented by tree spirits. Each species expresses its own wisdom through its form and growth. There are, for example, solid reliable oaks and adaptive flexible willows. Evergreens provide universal symbols for continuity. Holly, ivy and pine are still used to celebrate winter festivals. In Japan, a pine tree is placed at the back of the classical Japanese Noh stage to suggest eternal values. Evergreen pine branches (combined with bamboo and early plum blossoms) decorate household shrines at New Year to celebrate nature's resilience and continuity. A Japanese song celebrating the symbolic union of two pines is often (hopefully) requested to give a marriage an auspicious start.

Buddha is said to have found enlightenment under a Bo tree. Similarly, Jesus' story was linked with the concept of the tree of life through the legend of the True Cross, painted by Piero della Francesca. Ancient folkloric links with trees are revealed in characters such as the Green Man, still seen sprouting foliage from pub signs. The *I-Ching*, or Chinese 'Book of Changes', equates positive revolution or inevitable change with the natural way that deciduous trees drop their tired, exhausted leaves every autumn.

Fountains are also traditionally associated with perfect places. The antithesis of droughts and floods, they provide delightful sound effects and the visual equivalent of fireworks. Fountains, once nestling at the heart of mediaeval rose gardens or refreshing Moorish palaces on hot summer days, were given a lift by Tinguely. This artist's moving automatons (made of old iron and hose pipes) so delighted a *corps de ballet* that, when activated outside their Opera House, they leapt into the water to perform alongside their robotic neighbours. Fresh fountains and bubbling springs are symbols of joyous inspiration.

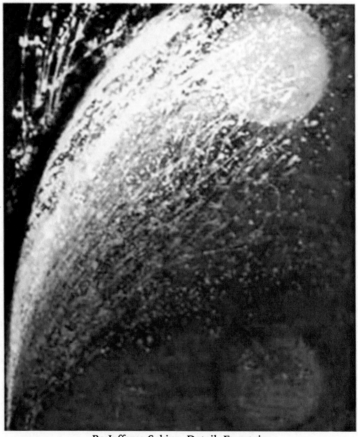

Bo Jeffares Sekine, Detail, Fountain

Bo Jeffares Sekine, Mutability

Symbols are continually shifted from one medium to the next. Paradise gardens exist in the mind, and are physically updated according to the skills and spatial possibilities of the times. They have inspired such varied works such as Livia's bird and flower filled mural from ancient Rome, the classical set piece at Stourhead, Pope's private garden, with its spiral circling a mound or the triangular cubist garden at Hyères. Definitions of paradise draw on private passions. Ideal spaces overlap images inspired by imagination and fact including books, pictures, travel, films, dreams and visions.

There are as many inspirational spaces as there are people. Some artists produce a range of varied landscapes. Pissarro was a modest man often called in to settle disputes between other fighting artists. He had an innate sense of calm and this permeates his work. Whether he was painting grand Parisian parks or simple rustic allotments he generated peace.

Parks provide crossover points between personal and public spaces. With increased urbanisation any green corner becomes precious. Lack of time, energy and funds restrict us and make guerrilla gardeners extra welcome. We need somewhere safe for small children to play, people to recuperate, relax, exercise, socialise, see trees, hear birds, smell flowers, watch insects, and experience nature's seasonal changes.

Outdoor spaces, such as the open air Yorkshire Sculpture Park, demonstrate a growing public desire to fuse art with nature. This park hosts sculpture by Henry Moore, Barbara Hepworth and Isamu Noguchi as well as some constructions by Andy Goldsworthy. This land artist promotes contemporary visions designed to make us to reflect on our relationship with the earth. Provocatively produced, perfectly placed, these works can push us to see nature from new angles, with new eyes.

Sophie Ryder created an '*Eye*' like an open air drawing, by bending galvanised metal rods to be seen against the luminous background of the sky. The sky spatially in-forms her art sited between natural tree shapes. Natural space and growth contribute context and meaning. It seems significant that, amongst many local and European agencies from the parish council upwards who support this creative space in Yorkshire, there is one which does not promote social or aesthetic issues, but trees themselves. It is symbolically entitled 'Trees for the Future'. A park like this helps us to re-view our relationship with the earth and consider what matters most for our future landscapes.

People say 'isn't it a small world?' Ideas about the size of the planet, or feelings about relative spaces adjust. We now live in a 'global village'. New York is just 'across the pond'. Exciting times when you could set off (hoping not to fall off the earth's outer rim) to found a new colony or preferential pilfering site have long evaporated. Modern man has mapped his world too well, though surprises may yet remain deep down in the oceans. Unexplored continents (populated by irrelevant indigenous types waiting to demonstrate their local cuisine before being efficiently exterminated) ideal dumping grounds for second sons, convicts, and adventurous free thinkers sadly no longer exist.

Travel seems easy, with adventure holidays packaged en-masse. Urban life, fluctuating in our imaginations between civilisation and decadence, is also criticised as unhealthy and unfriendly. The poet and artist, Blake, reacted with mystical wrath to industrialising pollution. Kafka cynically explored bureaucracy. But Beckett was the most succinct, playing out modern man's spiritual and spatial frustrations in *Waiting for Godot* (1955); two tramps in a pair of bins.

Imaginative authors, specifically those writing for or about children, love to juggle time and space. See Lewis Carroll's adaptation of a chess game to provide a flexible, surreal structure for *Alice's Adventures in Wonderland* (1865). Similarly, the philosophic choices later explored by Jostein Gaarder in *Sophie's World* in 1995 allow his readers to consider attitudes to reality. *Flatlands, A Romance in Many Dimensions* (1884) by Edwin A. Abbott provides the reader with multiple dimensions. It has adventures in Pointland (no dimensions), Lineland (one dimension), and Spaceland (three dimensions). Mathematical characters include the hero, A-square, plus circles, spheres and lines. Similar spatial adventures are explored in *Alice in Quantum Land* (1995), a laborious update of Carroll's earlier, quixotic fantasies.

Isabel Allende is a magical realist. In her thought-provoking novel *The House of Spirits* (1982), space is inhabited in many ways. This is traditional. Our ancestors frequently thought of their homes as clan centres, a central collection point for their ancestors. Household shrines are still presented with fresh food and drink worldwide so everyone feels included whether officially living or dead.

Bo Jeffares Sekine, House

Consider construction. A flat piece of ground, an 'empty' space, is intellectually manipulated by an architect. He incorporates practical engineering and aesthetic skills. He creates a layered spatial plan, visualising his blue-print. He moves, mentally, from foundations to roof tops, capturing or defining space. His project is materialised by a builder. This now solid, three dimensional area is then 'imaginatively' interpreted by a hopeful sales agent, intent on catching customers, by putting an imaginative gloss on the place. An impersonal box becomes inhabited. It evolves into a nucleus. A previously abstract space thus becomes a physical container for a family's hopes and dreams.

Coloured by the characteristics of its owners, a home starts to take on their emotional resonances absorbing its inhabitants' subjective 'atmosphere'. Rooms are associated with specific sensations. Set spaces are defined by particular actions or interactions. Comfortable, inquisitive, caring ghosts may not feel a need to move on. Some houses may shelter more inhabitants than officially stated in the Council Tax.

This is Allende's point in a nut shell. She describes a family space inhabited (in both physical and psychic senses) by more entities than meet the eye, and made all the richer for their interactive contributions. Her work deliberately challenges preconceptions about 'living spaces'. Allende, the South American interpreter of multiple realities, gave us her *House of Spirits*. Rachel Whiteread, an English concrete artist, filled a room with cement in 1990 to solidify or concretise a former living space. She called it *Ghost*. Both artists invite us to speculate on invisible links through time and place. Space holds more than oxygen and television waves. It can contain human imprints or memories. Explosive spaces, where people died in shock, can feel strangely cold. There seems to be a recurrent imprint of fear or displacement in such areas. 'Ordinary' dwelling places can absorb echoes of early occupants, popularising ghost tours for the Edinburgh Tourist Board.

Whiteread started casting objects, then spaces around them, then a room, then a complete house. She moves our attention from architectural structures to space itself. This is an invisible factor, or filling, within any structural conceit. Using the title *Ghost* focuses on such intangible qualities to evoke the past. Contained within this space many generations may have lived, and played out many dramas. Perhaps a room was a complete world for a pair of lovers, as John Donne poignantly suggests in his metaphysical poetry.

With *House* (1993), Whiteread links space with human life. This infilled building, space made matter, relates in her mind to the smallness and 'fragility of the spaces we actually live in, worry about, decorate all the things that are part of life'. *Place* (2008), shows a series of shells, or empty spaces relating to the places which we, like so many hermit crabs, scuttle in and out of. The sculptress presents us with a microcosmic collection of illuminated but empty dolls' houses indicating human isolation or abandonment.

Equally impersonally but more aggressively *Los Carpinteros*, The Carpenters, focus our attention on the violence present in everyday life. They destroy a room, filling its interior with shattering breeze blocks splintering impersonal, readymade furniture. Caught in time, like a cinematic still, the combined structural and utilitarian debris (carefully hung from transparent cords suspended from the ceiling), is disjointed, deliberately chaotic. *Show Room* (2008) shows an ideal space blowing asunder, disintegrating before our eyes. What we make to put on 'show' can be savagely destroyed at any time either by our own anarchy or natural disasters.

Fallen Star (2008) by the Korean Do Ho Suh, records his own internal shock or sense of disorientation when trying to adapt from Eastern space to Western space on starting to live in the USA. His old family home in Seoul, reproduced to a fifth of its normal size is physically crashed into the building he occupied in America, reproduced on its actual scale. His small, traditional, single-storey Korean house (with its traditional decorations and warm memories) crashes into the high, formal 18th or 19th century New England townhouse. This artist's belongings are mixed up, like his mind. His safe, secure, childhood space symbolically crashes into his new, exploratory student space. Debris lies around. It represents the psychological collision of his experimental opportunities within a new culture and nostalgic feelings for a former ideal or 'star' space.

It is a telling autobiographical image. The sculptor felt he had been emotionally pulled up and dropped by a tornado. Culture shock is recorded in three dimensions by this symbolic clash of two completely different living areas. *Fallen Star* is impersonal, (like a technically perfect Magritte) expressing shock without sound. It is dramatic on the outside, meticulous on the inside. There is great attention to detail (as in Proust). Everything is authentic and to scale, set within the right context and correct timescale. Pictures, posters, garments, kitchen equipment and a cat furnish this frozen theatre of the mind. The artist cuts through the fabric of this substantially layered American building, like a carpenter slicing up a doll's house.

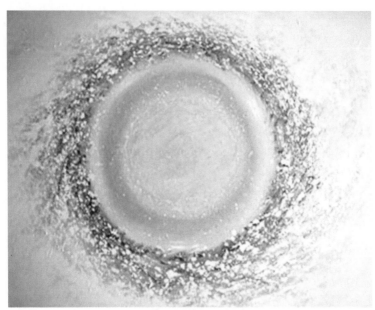

Bo Jeffares Sekine, Galaxy

Space, differently defined in East and West, is a keynote of this Korean artist's art work. His beloved childhood home was all doors and windows, lit by soft sunlight shining through pale, thin rice paper. He felt that contrasting enclosures in the USA seemed unattractively solid and opaque, as Western architects create an artificial kind of 'space totally separate from the outside' – from nature.

He tries to reinvent the essence of Korean architecture, which seems to him to be more permeable, 'more porous'. Hard boundaries and strict divisions lack mystery. Suh tries to suggest subtler effects in pared down 'material' works. Gauzy fabric, floating in the breeze, suggests a physical echo of early, inspirational spatial memories. These fabrications include sealed power cables, sockets and lights. The sculptor uses fabric to recreate physical spaces he has inhabited, such as a complete flat in New York, or a remembered flight of stairs. Stairs and ladders, often used as symbols for spiritual ascension, are luminously updated.

Bo Jeffares Sekine, Detail, Ascension

The past provides the foundations for the future. Attached to his memories, Suh wants to take them with him, like a snail travelling with its shell. The artist wants to move with his past, which is such a strong part of his identity. And he does. Packed up in a suitcase (imagine the scene at customs' checks) he carries the literally 'fabricated' spaces he loves so much around with him, explaining 'I have a longing for this particular space and I want to recreate that space, or bring that space, wherever I go'.

Translucent rooms shifting in the air, sewn in soft, suspended fabrics are the technical opposite to Whiteread's hard, solid blocks. Not concrete but, in his words, 'intangible, metaphysical, and psychological'. Needing some kind of physical substance to define his dreams, he has settled for 'borrowing material that renders the idea of transparency', like Shakespeare's 'baseless fabric' evoked at the conclusion of *The Tempest*, he conjures up an ethereal essence.

Tomas Saraceno, an imaginative futurist from Argentina, develops the idea of a transparent city space. This flexible living space would be moved by the elements 'like a cloud'. Changing its construction, fusing, fluid, floating, able to merge with similar city platforms, this city would mysteriously metamorphose 'just as clouds do'.

This nomadic city space driven by its social needs would embrace the latest technology. It would illustrate creative processes at work. For, just as we envisaged air travel and then invented it physically, many visionary dreams or wonders from science 'fiction' gradually manifest in reality. Imaginative ideals take shape to become accepted elements in the material world. As an early part of this dream in the sky, Saracento created a 'real' air bubble, a space where people can see and be seen as if weightless above the ground. *Observatory, Air-port-city* (2008) illustrates that ideas about ideal places, or utopias are in 'constant mutation'. Architects in Australia are currently discussing the concept of floating cities as a practical means of conserving ground space for food production.

Sometimes we don't see the wood for the trees. We need to step back to put things in perspective or try to get a more rounded view. Isamu Noguchi achieved this. With East/West parentage, this versatile creator was able to combine aesthetic gifts and traditions from both sides of the world. He learnt to create international abstractions. Just as many architects creatively envisage space, so Noguchi creatively appreciated space and spatial effects. He equated sculpture with the perception of space, calling it the very 'continuum of our existence.'

Space is a shared factor in everyone's lives. In Japan, where flat land is limited, people are extremely conscious of space, both personally and socially. They may have anticipated the living problems of future generations. Japanese aesthetics are often worked out in terms of spaces rather than scale or objects. There is a traditional interest in space for its own sake, with sounds or objects used to break up spatial progressions. Noguchi was intrigued by relative spaces, and the flow of space between objects.

Noguchi's understanding of people's reactions to space is seen in his indoor *Heaven* in Tokyo. His use of space, and creation of particular feelings in particular sites, could be compared with other creative figures, such as Shakespeare, who had enjoyed playing with many spatial possibilities. Shakespeare's magician created a magic ring, as a dramatic device, to hold people captive in *The Tempest*. This was a poetically charged space. Similarly, in 1970, Noguchi shaped stone to encapsulate space in his *Magic Ring*. He described this as a 'ring of containment, something magic. Merlin drew it in sand'. All artists are magicians, working to make us sense space or question reality anew.

This sculptor (linking his East/West inheritance) sought unity in universal symbols such as the circle. This abstract form represents an archetypal closing or enclosing device. It always has peaceful, idealistic overtones. Circles are endlessly adapted. See the stone circles built by pagan ancestors, the concentric rings of Asian Mandalas or universe symbols, round buildings such as the Pantheon in Rome (generously built for all religions) or environmental green belts encircling our cities. Cohesive 'round table' discussions (as championed by King Arthur, Native Americans, and contemporary business brains) and linking circle dances (as portrayed by Breughel and Matisse) help to maintain social harmony. Circles sum up cycles of action. Spirals portray evolutionary patterns. Light reflects love.

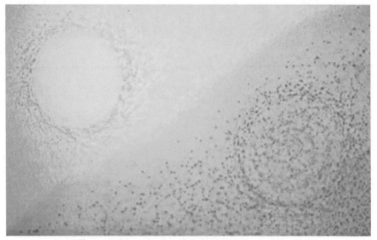

Bo Jeffares Sekine, Sun and Spiral/ Light and Evolution

Artists employ shapes and symbols to charge sites with special significance, or positive energy, like all of us carefully creating stress free areas at home and at work. Intangible feelings in places may be hard to define, but we intuitively sense subtle differences.

Shakespeare was adept at evoking such spatial ambiguities. What is solid, what is not? – 'we are such stuff as dreams are made of'. He frequently teases our imagination into new realms. Parallel progressions, from mind to matter are made real in Velazquez's painting *The Fable of Arachne*, also called 'The Spinners' (1611). Here a sophisticatedly understated painter leads the mind's eye through several levels of existence from the ordinary to the extraordinary.

Shifts in perception, from the everyday to the mystic, are anticipated and indeed consciously catered for by skilled Japanese artists. Zen monks program our minds to change gear, to move from the mundane to the metaphysical. Deliberately layered spatial effects in Zen Gardens are designed to increase esoteric consciousness, and lead to a feeling of unity with the whole of the universe.

Noguchi drew on these Eastern values. He responded to space as a natural vehicle for an intuitive understanding of the cosmos. Excited by the idea that sculpture can create spatial effects and form psychological illusions, he consciously cultivated its magical, or mystical potential. Shapes intended for this purpose, when properly scaled could, he said, 'actually create a greater space'. Tellingly, he adds that there is a difference between logical space, which can be measured in cubic feet, and the 'additional space that the imagination supplies. One is the measure, the other an awareness of the void – joint existence in this passing world'.

His spatial consciousness (like that of Allende in *The House of Spirits*) informed his work whatever media he was using whether heavy or light, paper or stone. He respected the planet's basic elements, constructing with water and rock. His respect for the earth herself was balanced by curiosity about space. When he was asked to form a modern adaptation of Seneca's *Phaedra*, he decided to update Hippolytus by placing him in a space capsule. 'He is the cosmonaut, his eyes on the stars'.

This symbolic spaceman, in his silver cocoon, anticipated a later desire to make a monument to the spacecraft Challenger.

Noguchi was an artist looking out, trying to raise consciousness and encourage our appreciation of the wonders of outer space. He mirrored the sky in still pools cut into stone tables. He evoked deep space with vast works entitled *Void* or *Portal*. Perhaps adapting the old Shintoist idea of a Torii, or wide open spirit gate, he made new, minimalist, modern doorways. Their smooth, impersonal frames dwarf us. One massive structure rising high on metal legs or stilts was entitled *Sky Gate*.

In the eighteenth century sophisticated travellers would carry a Claude glass – an instant framing apparatus for enclosing a perfect vista. This created instant contained, classical landscapes, inspired by the balanced scenic views of the classical painter Claude Lorraine. Noguchi, however, directed attention not along a horizontal plane, but up and out. He was intent on focusing our mind's eye through his *Sky Gate* to the void and beyond to evoke 'the continuum of our existence,' pure space.

Spatial decisions sum up a civilisation's preoccupations. Satellite, geophysical and archaeological evidence often reveals how beliefs shape reality. Ancient Athens devoted prime space to public arenas to promote free speech as a physical reflection of its growing democratic idealism.

In some cases 'past' and 'future' can overlap. George Lucas filmed a slave city of the future in an ancient, ethnic part of Tunisia when creating his science fiction epic *Star Wars* in 1977. Cities exist as solid, physical realities, remembered through town planning and quantity surveyors' data, and also on a more metaphysical level.

Alexandria was famed for its prosperous market and renowned for its international library. Ideas, as well as objects, were exchanged and traded. Books in passing boats were conscientiously copied for the great library. Intellectuals were welcomed as well as merchants. Alexandria became associated with cosmopolitan exoticism, as in Durrell's later tribute, written between1957 and 1960, *The Alexandria Quartet*.

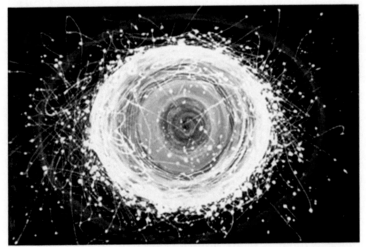

Bo Jeffares Sekine, Space

The Italian writer Italo Calvino takes this kind of cultural mythology one stage further in his novel *The Invisible City* (1972). This atmospheric exploitation of overlapping utopian visions has evocative chapter headings such as 'Cities and Memory' or 'Continuous Cities'. Tides of past and the future pull us backwards and forwards as hopes and memories shape consciousness and fuel creation.

Popular imagination seizes on specific monuments as clues to a city's character, just as we isolate particular features to sum up someone's personality. Thus Berlin's broken barrier or Paris' Eiffel Tower sum up the political pain or romantic escapism associated with these specific capitals. Each city generates its own myth. It has its own spatial keys, or panoramic viewing spots, tourist magnets like the London Eye.

Each future space city will provide a microcosm of its social attitudes. All its power struggles will be expressed in terms of its spatial priorities. Not only in apportioning quantities of space, but also in selecting dominant sites and positions for specific purposes, setting up relative juxtapositions within its central areas. Planners crystallise their motivation. The space a city gains and reconstructs recounts the story of its life.

Physical and metaphysical merge as Lorenzetti demonstrated when using town planning to depict allegories of good and bad government in Sienna. Solid components and structures are increasingly overtaken by hidden supply and transport systems such as the underground. There is an expansion of what Isozaki, in his famous 'City Invisible' Essay of 1966, called a 'combination of invisible systems'. Traditional cities built of stone and brick and burning fossil fuels are superseded by modern centres made of new, structural components running on electromagnetic energy and solar power.

Visible and invisible energies permeate our activities. They blur boundaries between what is 'real' and what is 'unreal'. Each person decides what is real or surreal for them as they experiment to form blue prints for future creations.

The ancient Greeks selected Delphi, 'the navel of the world', as a suitable site for an oracle. This huge complex included sports facilities and concealed subterranean compartments. People literally remained in the dark, fasting or taking drugs before viewing staged revelations spun by their contemporary spin doctors. In 1889, modern Americans, also toying with the occult, adapted a games format in a popular film. Eternal desires to experiment with as yet unclassified realities are explored in *Field of Dreams.*

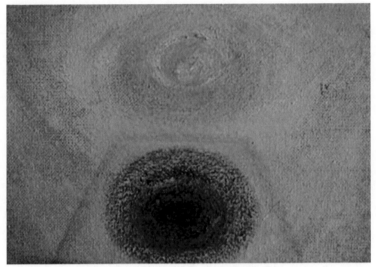

Bo Jeffares Sekine, Dream Field

A farmer is dream-inspired to build a baseball pitch in his fields. This serves as a symbolic space, at once natural and supernatural. Dead baseball players including his own father are able to perform here. A game field has been created with an extra psychic dimension. Here time is flexible and emotional reconciliation finally becomes possible. This is symbolised by the hero's decision to join the other players, whom he has been instrumental in reuniting, as they enact their shared dreams. They play together harmoniously in imaginative space as realities blend to foster a seamless solution.

Dreams provide ideal links between different realities. Dreams can link everyday survival with spiritual or transcendental experiences. In our dreams, time, space and gravity are always fluid, always magically flexible.

Picasso described all art as a form of magic. He was superstitious. Art's role, including the concentration of thought into form, has always been cultivated as a means of sourcing, shaping and processing life's mysteries. Neolithic hunting processions depicted on cave walls, and richly equipped tombs, remind us of the creative energy poured into concretising our ancestors' hopes for future happiness by recording positive images.

Significantly, Chin, the Chinese emperor who chose to be buried with his huge terracotta army, symbolising physical protection from resentful enemies, also wanted to be interred with a linked map of sky and earth. This double map symbolised celestial and domestic unity. This ruler 'read' the skies for practical reasons, just as recent governments employ satellite photos for mutual spying purposes. His double earth and space map was complete with flowing rivers composed of silvery mercury, moving mechanically to seem more 'realistic' Accuracy was essential for knowledge, and knowledge was synonymous with power.

In the Chinese imagination at that time the sky was considered a mirror of the earth. Trouble in the skies meant trouble at home; 'as above, so below'. So meteors, eclipses and unprecedented star movements were systematically studied to alert the emperor to potential problems within the provinces. People 'saw' the heavens as a reflection of their own earthly bureaucracy. Rather than looking modestly to the heavens for inspiration, as superior spaces, they were more preoccupied with their own, engrossing concerns. The vast Milky Way was described as a 'path across the mountains', and Hayley's Comet familiarly equated with a 'Broom Star'.

Bo Jeffares Sekine, Red Italy

Art, including abstract art, is continuously sparked by such
sentiments. Core beliefs fuel creative experiments. Picasso saw,

or defined, his world as strange and hostile. Consequently his vision reflected fear and aggression. Women were either goddesses or doormats, in that order.

Searching for meanings in life, Picasso referred to art as a 'mediator' between the world and humanity. Image-making for him was more of a disconnected activity than a social one. Contrast so-called 'primitive' artists whose life and work expresses tribal beliefs through imagery designed to harmonise and inspire the whole community. Art was imaginatively employed to connect us with other life forms. Symbols were created to link us with the rest of life. Native American cultures, for example, created the myth of 'Grandmother Spider', a karmic entity in the centre of the web of life evoked to help with healing rites. She traditionally teaches the mysteries of the past to reveal current consequences. What we think about now seeds the future.

Spiders spinning are reminders of everyone's creative potential. Spiders can symbolise language teaching and the intricacies of writing. A spider's body, its two main joined up circular sections, resembles the infinity symbol found in mathematics. This horizontal figure-of-eight often symbolises continuous energy flow. Like the serpentine curve flowing through asymmetric Eastern *yin/yang* symbols, it expresses a perfect balance between active and passive or male and female energies.

America's ancient Medicine Wheels were set up to harmonise visible and invisible energies. These landscaped centres, early earth art, were conceived as power points to focus and attract cosmic energy, to ground us and connect us with the universe at large.

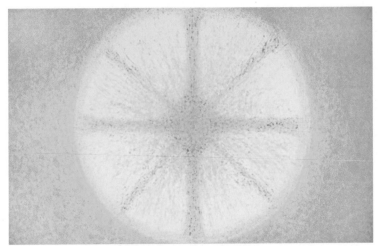

Medicine Wheel/Celtic Cross

Celtic Crosses provide another visual unit designed to sum up balance within and without. Like Medicine Wheels, these crosses can refer to the four equidistant compass points – North, South, East and West. In old Cornish carvings a central figure often embodies the cross. Sacred geometry becomes personalised. A body with outstretched arms, grounded feet, and head nearer to the sky becomes a symbol of Heaven on Earth.

Peter Doig, the Canadian artist, fuses earth and space in his *Milky Way* (1889-90). Inspired by a dream sequence, he paints a river of stars flowing across the top of his canvas and also reflected in a line along its base as though mirrored in still water. Between these 'real' and 'reflected' stars he paints a line of trees, sandwiched in a cosmic perspective.

This landscapist is another artist who has evolved beyond national boundaries. He tries to create limitless images about us all 'living on the planet.'

Spatial Games

We focus on what interests us. Art works contribute when they play with space to allow us to flex our mental muscles. Space, something we all share, provides a good medium for aesthetic comparisons whether we are dealing with words, paint or plants. Shakespeare employed literary genius. Velasquez developed visual powers. Japanese tea masters used subtle landscaping tricks. All these works help to open new mental doors.

In an actual three dimensional site such as a garden composed of growing trees and solid pathways we can experience space directly. Our senses are engaged. We move around and appreciate elements such as scented plants, herbs, fruits and berries, the sound of the wind in the trees, the gurgle of running water, and colour. There are also illusionary landscapes. Shakespeare's illusion, for groundlings and philosophers alike, of an imaginary sea-bound island in *The Tempest* (1611) is no geographical reality. Evoked with words, sounds and movements, Shakespeare's fantasy is recreated anew by successive producers, actors and audiences. Their combined actions and reactions move our minds from the escapist venue of the theatre into yet more intangible realms.

Moving from poetry to painting, Velasquez provides a play within a play. Constructing a visual parable for the human condition, he links tangible and intangible levels of life by fusing the real with the surreal. Our ordinary every-day world and our mythical or magic-making capacities are interwoven in *The Fable of Arachne*. Sheep's fleeces are physically spun and woven in a picture also interwoven with ideas about transformation. Our creative endeavours allow us to rival the gods. Arachne, a mythical weaver, was a highly skilled woman whose arts rivalled those of the Greek Gods. She has become a prototype for everyone using their ingenuity to express their imaginative potential.

Balanced between earth and sky (like our own existence) this theatrical scene concentrates on down-to-earth-facts, lumpy fleeces in a dark factory, highlighting its more fantastical elements. Deep blacks, dusty browns, and warm, rusty reds create a heavy, earthy quality in a spatial enclosure designed to set off a more transparent inner image featuring clear, transparent sky and open space. This is an art work within an art work. A colourful tapestry shown off in this gloomy workshop catches our eyes, drawing us into spatial speculation.

Different creators transform everyday factors into inspirational ones by adapting staged experiments or spatial sequences. Serious scientists explain that matter can logically be transformed into energy, as with Einstein's famous formula is $E=mc^2$. Intuitive artists can also transform our perception of simple matters into miraculous moulds. They adapt aesthetics. Occasionally great art works try to deal with or explain the whole creative process. These explore interlocking levels of being. They contain clues to the whole process of detachment, the alchemical abstraction of ordinary life into philosophic visions. The best scientists, like Einstein, are aware of intuition's role in exploring and defining reality. As Einstein said 'Imagination is everything. It is the preview of life's coming attractions'.

Klee stated that art does not reproduce the visible, but it 'renders visible'. The best artworks reveal eternal truths. Art reveals the

Bo Jeffares Sekine, Inner Stage

hidden, greater or timeless values so often obscured by all the fuss and bother of daily lives. We usually see life through a glass, darkly. Art however can provide glimpses of holistically linked, invisible realms previously the preserve of mystics (not the most communicative of figures).

Creating art can be a process of refinement, a revealing of symbols. Means and methods can be juxtaposed or flexibly interchanged as artists try to interpret life by finding sounds, colours, shapes, and above all symbols to explain their individual approaches to existence. Artists provide us with fast food for spiritual evolution. Absorbing pre-packaged images we can creatively leapfrog ahead.

In *The Tempest* Shakespeare invents a site to suit his subtleties. The dramatist magically manipulates each aspect of reality. Concealing, controlling, revealing, he places his characters in spatial situations to suit, or check, their evolution. Manoeuvring them like pawns, he makes use of this tailored landscape to separate his separate different strands of reality.

The Fable of Arachne provides a visual parable where Velazquez employs a similar spatial strategy. He uses a frozen time scale. The painter employs a stage-like set with a mythical backdrop. Simultaneously drawing our attention to different degrees of artistry, he develops our perception of different strands of truth.

Landscaping, architecture and related arts enhance the Japanese tea ceremony. They permit creators to play with spatial progression on varied physical planes. The tea ceremony, however, differs from the painting and the play just mentioned in that guests are more involved. When invited to a tea ceremony they are neither viewers nor audience but participants in a ceremony designed to transform daily life into an art form.

The tea master, like a theatre director or film producer, harmonises all the elements within his overall production to unify everything within his cultural remit. Selecting an image such as a calligraphic script, or nature-inspired ink drawing, he provides an imaginative focus for his guests.

Their appreciative comments, often expressed in stylised poems, add their own reflections. By his choice and arrangement of food, pottery and flowers as well as his interior and exterior designs, he attempts an overall aesthetic. Noted qualities are grace and modesty rather than lavish ostentation. Refined juxtapositions reveal understated taste just as Zen masters praise 'poverty surpassing riches.'

A similar sentiment is expressed in *The Tempest* where Shakespeare states: 'Most poor matters Point to rich ends' (I11, – 3, 4). Very often poor materials can be transformed into rich results, as with the *arte povera* movement inspiring modern earth artists.

Materials may be rich in the imaginative sense of arousing metaphysical speculation. *The Tempest*, like *A Midsummer Night's Dream* (1595), combines human beings with other versions of life. But whereas the former's supernatural elements increase the play's comic scope, the elemental spirits driving *The Tempest* work a very different kind of magic: Ariel and his ilk can be seen as instruments of fate or destiny.

Ariel himself, sometimes seen sometimes secret, whets our appetite for the invisible forces in life. The elements themselves are frequently conjured up as part of the play's raw materials. See how the guilty king repeatedly envisages himself in a significantly dirty, or muddy, grave. Earth and water are constantly evoked, as are sea and sky. Prospero the magician stages his elemental 'war' between the 'green sea and the azured vault'. He also adapts the classic image of the tree of life portraying himself as a victim whose vitality was sucked out by his parasitic brother.

This is the duke's metaphor for his brother's usurpation of his political power. Prospero states that his sibling was

> The ivy which had hid my princely trunk,
> And sucked my verdure out on't (I, ii, 85–7)

Later when suggesting the king's death by drowning, Ariel also adapts natural imagery, by singing of an amazing 'sea change', a transformation indicating a metamorphosis into something 'rich and strange'

> Of his bones are coral made;
> Those are pearls that were his eyes. (I, ii, 401–2)

Bo Jeffares Sekine, Sky, Sea and Land

The bare bones of Shakespeare's tale become precious. He transmutes base matter into poetry, just as rough grit can be smoothed into translucent spheres: 'Those are pearls that were his eyes', a phrase later woven into T.S. Eliot's poem *The Waste Land*.

Images of fire and air enliven Shakespeare's play, as evinced by Ariel's delight in filling the ship with flashes of fire, and happily manipulating thunder and lightning to terrify people. An air spirit, capable of transforming himself into a water sprite, he describes his breathtaking transitions including an ability to fly,

> To swim, to dive into the fire not, to ride
> On the curled clouds (I, ii, 191–3)

There are strong parallels between the elements and the personalities in this play. We all know the relief after a storm has passed causing the lowering of electrical pressure. Shakespeare makes the most of a tempest's power to stir up tension, to create a similar psychological storm within his characters' hearts. Thus the traumatic, physical wrecking and subsequent soul-searching lead in the end to the proverbial calm after the storm, symbolically secured by Ferdinand and Miranda's forthcoming marriage.

When Ferdinand is first washed up, shipwrecked and seemingly all alone on the island shore, he voices these parallels. Ariel's melody simultaneously soothes the sea's rough waves to calm his mind.

> This music crept by me upon the waters,
> Allaying both their fury and my passion
> With its sweet air. (I, ii, 3–7)

Shakespeare's concept of co-existing realities is staged within the microcosmic resources of *The Tempest*. Ostensibly, he observes the dramatic concept of the Three Unities, the classic interconnection of time, place and action. These imply that the actions of his drama would have taken place (roughly) within the time scale of his performance, and that the territory described could have been traversed within (roughly) the same time scale. But, as he is employing spirits to chivvy his actors around, no normal rules apply. Moved and magnetised by music, these shipwrecked travellers' adventures are in fact masterminded by the magician Prospero, from their first decision to jump ship right up to their final reunion.

Bo Jeffares Sekine, Energy Island

Spatially, Shakespeare's island is large enough to allow him to sequester and isolate separate groups. He discreetly hides the ship in an inlet, keeping the crew asleep below decks until they are required for the return journey. With the sailors conveniently out of the way, the king and his courtiers can explore the island searching for Prince Ferdinand. Meanwhile the subplot unites three buffoons (a foolish jester, a drunken butler and a sadly disgruntled savage, the bestial but exploited Caliban). Ferdinand is hypnotically lured to meet Miranda Prospero's charming daughter. When Prospero commands Ariel to hold his enemies in check, this spirit draws on the island's landscape potential – having experienced it at first hand, himself, imprisoned in a tree for twelve years by its previous occupant, a witch.

Ariel's manoeuvres vary. This adds to the play's dramatic propensity. It also mirrors the complexity of Shakespeare's audiences. First produced before the court, this play appealed to highly cosmopolitan minds and also less educated, earthy tastes.

Consequently the different levels of reality accessed within the play, from coarse slapstick to sophisticated artifice, reflect the range of its original audience. Simpler characters are ridiculed for crude comedy, as Ariel sticks them in the mud, or chases them with dogs. More aristocratic characters experience more complex charades. Ariel metamorphoses into a vengeful harpy, abandons them to suffer in a grove, and confines them within a magic circle. This symbolic spatial device, in which Prospero reveals the truth and achieves a much needed reconciliation, concludes this whole cycle of events.

Distanced from this conclusion, both mentally (since they had no part in causing the original problems) and physically, the lovers remain outside the main action. Prospero's original plan, that they would fall in love and marry, is then revealed. He draws a curtain to reveal a concealed, inner space, and shares his vision of the young lovers together. This produces a cameo effect. They are seen playing a game of chess within the magician's cell their obvious accord generating love and suggesting a hopeful marriage of true minds.

Moods and memories inform this piece, a landscape game on several levels. The inclusion of the word 'maze' seems telling. Used by the king, amazed by his experiences on the magic island, this maze image reinforces the idea of a puzzle. There was a maze constructed at Hampton Court in 1608. Elizabethans knew of the legendary maze or labyrinth housing the Minotaur in classical mythology. Classical references abound. Two elaborate masques add to an already dramatic spectacle.

Pageants add to the range of incongruous figures populating the island. Strange spirits and dignified divinities enrich the cast's diversity. Ariel is helped by silent beings whose miming helps to confuse and disorient the king's party. A set of supernatural beings bless the lovers' betrothal. Prospero, the stage director, uses this display to demonstrate his abilities. There is a celebratory dance between nymphs and reapers, speeches by Ceres, the goddess of the harvest, and Juno the goddess of marriage. Juno descends from the heavens, as goddesses should. Iris, her celestial messenger, personifies a rainbow, a traditional symbol of peace, or light bridge linking heaven and earth.

Bo Jeffares Sekine, Rainbow Bridge

Bridging fact and fantasy like this, Shakespeare can dissolve logical boundaries. Miranda, the sailors, and the king are put to sleep at will. Dreams are easily evoked. Caliban pays touching tribute to his enchanted home, an isle of hypnotic melodies:

> Sounds and sweet airs, that give delight, and hurt not.
> Sometimes a thousand twangling instruments
> Will hum about mine ears; and sometime voices,
> That, if I then had waked after long sleep,
> Will make me sleep again. And then, in dreaming,
> The clouds methought would open, and show riches
> Ready to drop upon me; that, when I waked,
> I cried to dream again. (III, ii, 128–136)

Dreams provide a flexible, indeterminate state. Are they a halfway house between life and death? Portraying psychological as well as spatial dimensions the playwright prompts us to ask: what is real and what illusion? Just as the physical action in his story, the maritime adventure and discoveries of his travellers, corresponds to contemporary explorations, so the metaphysical musings of his magician, based on the contemporary alchemist Dr. Dee, encourage a questioning approach to life.

Shakespeare produces a play within a play. As Prospero's performance concludes, he makes his mouthpiece say that his pageant has been built of ethereal material or 'baseless fabric'. His sorcerer adds that the earth and its inhabitants can similarly dissolve away. He concludes that we are such stuff

> As dreams are made on; and our little life
> Is rounded with a sleep. (IV, iii, 156–8)

This play, like most comedies of forgiveness, provides a blueprint for content. Forgiveness nurtures love, to dissolve grief. Prospero forgives himself, accepting that he should not have become so enthralled by his studies that he neglected his worldly responsibilities. So he works in the present to try to redress this balance. He tries to cultivate compassion. He forgives his enemies. Possible rape and murder averted, he becomes less resentful. He will later seek forgiveness for his sins from us, his audience. By praying for him, we activate mercy which, by a creative chain reaction, also frees our own hearts and minds.

The Tempest concludes with a play on the way in which faith can build into reality. Prospero, Shakespeare's magical mouthpiece, makes a distinct parallel between his former supernatural powers over the other players and the audience's hold over him. He asks for applause, as a positive sign that we approve of his actions. Our energy will transport him to the mainland. He asks to be symbolically released from the island 'by your spell'. So as we direct our energies we too become creative magicians.

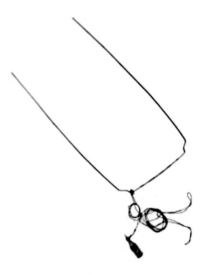

Bo Jeffares Sekine, Acrobat

Staged Effects

Just as writers create different speech rhythms to suggest contrasting emotional wavelengths, adjusting poetry and prose, varying idioms and vocabulary, so painters manipulate colours, tones and shapes. Thus, where Shakespeare contrasted crude and subtle scenes verbally, Velazquez created distinct painterly contrasts within his visual 'fabric'. He carefully juxtaposed down-to-earth and illusionistic imagery. Working within a fixed timescale, the artist distilled his metaphor for the entire creative process into a single dynamic unit, overlapping layers of myth and meaning.

Unlike a play, recreated anew with each production, or a unique tea ceremony, Velazquez's image of *The Fable of Arachne* remains a constant. It is mysterious. Braque once said that every painting had something inexplicable about it, and that this was its best bit. Velazquez' picture is full of best bits.

Just as Socrates taught by asking questions rather than indoctrinating, so Velazquez's subtle ambiguities provoke curiosity. His heroine, Arachne was a spinner and a weaver, fulfilling a traditionally creative female role. Unmarried women, devoid of family responsibilities, were called spinsters. If their creativity wasn't going into reproduction it was traditionally diverted into cloth. Arachne is the archetypal weaver, Velazquez's potent symbol for the artist in anyone. She was punished for her creative presumption and brilliance by Athene, the Greek goddess of wisdom. Velasquez shows his heroine providing a lively challenge to this divine rival.

Arachne the legendary spinner and weaver accepted Athene's challenge to produce a set of competitive works. The woman cheekily selected subject-matter designed to undermine the gods' supposed moral authority. She accurately presented Athene's father, Zeus, as a rapist. She recorded the time when Zeus disguised himself as a bull to seduce and rape a trusting woman called Europa. Truth hurts. Athene hated this negative 'spin'. She was annoyed. She retaliated. Exercising damage-control, her lowly rival was allowed to continue spinning for eternity, but as a mere insect. Arachne, her name now synonymous with spiders, became demoted to one of the humblest spinners.

By selecting this classical myth, Velazquez parallels literary creativity; *ut pictura poesis*. He visualises an episode from Ovid's *Metamorphoses*. He also incorporates a reference to a work by the famous Italian painter Titian then available for him to see and study in Spain. By including a subtle evocation of Titian's *Rape of Europa* (1562), Velasquez implies that Arachne's work was, indeed, of the highest possible inventive standard. By visualising this challenge between a creative mortal and a temperamental goddess, Velazquez hints at art's ability to transcend plain weaving and fabricate mythology.

Early images reveal him starting to juxtapose physical surfaces, such as the earthy roughness of pottery compared with the translucent transparency of glass. In *Old Woman Frying Eggs* (1618), he chooses to capture a second of physical transition, as heat solidifies liquid egg whites. His image provides a simple example of homely alchemy or easily recognised domestic change. *Old Woman Frying Eggs* also provides a physical contrast between youth and age, as the rough texture of the old cook's wrinkled face acts as a counterpoint to the smooth skin of the observant young boy. Such scenes anticipate later, more intellectually demanding paintings employing much subtler visual contrasts.

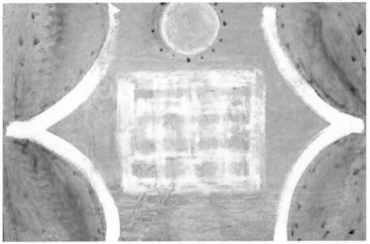

Bo Jeffares Sekine, Staged Effects

In his parable *Christ in the House of Martha and Mary* (c.1622), Velazquez offsets worldly and ethical values. Traditional tensions are usually felt between philosophic listeners and practical activists. These differences are implied by two disconnected areas within his picture. Each illusion of a separate space heightens the value of the other. Within this shared dwelling contrasting rooms reveal opposite mindsets. 'Within my house are many mansions.'

The foreground or primary scene dominates in *Christ in the House of Martha and Mary*. However the secondary or background scene provides a telling comment. A still, or flash-back, incorporated into a film, or the inclusion of a dream sequence in a Noh play, adds another dimension to a major theme, giving it a wider spiritual perspective. In this painting Velazquez paints two women in his realistic foreground, an older one despairing, a younger one grumpy. The young woman is preparing food. She is associated with an unpretentious, factual still life. Domesticity is summed up by her mortar and pestle, a red pepper, garlic, and eggs on a plate. Crisply painted kitchen close-ups are contrasted with a far-off scene enacted in a rectangle cut from the dark background. It provides a window on the action, to add spatial and moral perspective. Blurred to seem distant, this inner chamber reveals Jesus talking to Martha and Mary. Is he advocating the value of wisdom over housework?

In a subsequent work *The Family of Philip IV* (1656), he plays at challenging or reversing the accepted social order. He relegates the king and queen (whom he was no doubt officially painting) to a distant, observatory role. These powerful figures are placed firmly at the back of his composition, faintly reflected in a distant mirror. The artist also includes himself as an enigmatic figure standing at the side of his composition. Tantalisingly, we are only shown the back of his huge canvas. It is a deliberately concealed image. We want to yank it round. What we can see are records of authentic contemporaries, royal patrons, courtiers, a young princess, small dwarfs and large dogs.

The Fable of Arachne has a more intriguing cast, and subtler spatial ambiguities. Space here includes physical, theatrical and mythical dimensions. Velazquez's foreground equates with a factory floor, but his furthest distances become ever more gently nuanced.

This appears dark. But close scrutiny is rewarding. Within this earthy, brown darkness with its patches of red, a huge russet curtain is pulled back theatrically, like the curtain in *The Tempest*, to reveal an inner room. This device focuses our attention on a large, stage or inner room with silkily clad ladies, plus images of Athene and Arachne. Velazquez creates an inset or masque here. This provides another interpretation, adds another level of meaning, to the factual processes taking place in the foreground. One of the aristocratic visitors looks directly at us, pulling our attention into this central area.

Colour also leads our attention inwards. Deep rusty reds are displaced by brighter hues, light canary yellow and clear blues. The eye is pulled inwards, as Velazquez lightens his tones to create a pale, pastel sky. There are no spatial challenges from open doors or windows. Velazquez blacks them out. A dramatic spotlight (a shaft of sunlight from some high, hidden source) focuses attention on this final evocation of limitless space.

For generations after his death Velazquez's picture was known as '*The Spinners*'. People appreciated it on a factual level. Because

Diego Velasquez, 'The Spinners'

he was in no way obvious with this allegory, many failed to see his finer allusions. But that is its charm. This is no crude fairground piece. It is the antithesis of the kind of landscape, found at the seaside where we physically insert our heads, if not our minds. Velazquez is succinct. He edits, for example, an early 'fat lady' at the beach, Titian's well-built Europa. He just leaves a discreet reference to her billowing drapery. He cuts out the bull (or action) completely. His interest appears to lie in space itself. Mythical space then, like cyberspace now, was a flexible means of stretching the parameters of reality. Like minimalist Zen scenes selected to inspire the mood of a tea ceremony, or the 'borrowed vistas' employed to stretch the eye outwards in Japanese gardens, Velazquez borrows a vista. He creates an artwork within an artwork, by adding a visual quotation. Just as ore is smelted into metal, or grapes fermented into wine, then distilled into brandy, so matter is processed into art.

Arachne herself symbolises this kind of gradual development. She was professionally accomplished in all aspects of her craft. She could card, spin, dye and design. Her raw material, sheep's wool, is seen unprocessed in lumps on the factory floor. Spinning and carding is also taking place. And in the far distance, in the further salon, we have a glimpse of a richly coloured, embroidered tapestry. Velazquez apparently based aspects of his composition on an existing factory, giving his picture a degree of authenticity. Rather than an ordinary weaver's workshop, this was part of a highly sophisticated industry dedicated to transposing designs into subtle, woven mediums frequently preferred to paintings, and often more expensive. Velasquez's choice of a mythical theme reinforces his interest in the many stages or sequences of creative processes.

Such processes are paralleled by the dramatis personae involved. Just as Shakespeare suggests a whole range of realities by moving from the bestial to the supernatural (from Caliban, that 'deboshed fish', to Ariel, a synchronistic expression of Prospero's desires) so Velazquez's personnel is inspiring, and varied. An artist keen to promote his own social worth, he includes workers, possible customers, and allegorical figures. This range represents the depth and resources of his interior, creative world.

Like the artist, Shakespeare can be deliberately ambiguous. In his Epilogue to *The Tempest*, delivered by Prospero, the audience knows that the play is being wound up. They know that the actors have concluded the action. Yet Prospero never exactly says: 'I am an actor, and that was a fantasy'. The magician continues, instead, to refer to himself as the Duke of Milan, begging the audience's support to help him to find the way home. Is Shakespeare saying that if we believe in Prospero he is 'real' as belief creates reality? Our energy, our creative interactions with his fantasies, gives them substance, lends them validity or life.

Similarly, does Velazquez want us to see Athene and Arachne as mythical figures, or real in the sense of being like us? If they were in the tapestry, surely the thick embroidered panel framing this work would also be continued along the floor line? Yet there is an insubstantiality about the hemline and solidity of Arachne's dress. Are she and the armoured goddess actually standing in the same physical space as the three aristocratic women? Within this baroque conceit, the older woman at the spinning wheel is also thought to represent Athene, flashing a nubile leg as a clue to her disguise.

Just as Prospero refers to Miranda as the 'thread' linking his life together, so the spider's capacity to spin and weave is continually reinterpreted. We speak of weaving in and out of the dance of life, encapsulated in Yeats' line 'How can I tell the dancer from the dance?' We refer to sad, threadbare days, the fabric of life, the warp and weft of existence, picking up the thread of a relationship, homespun wisdom, seamless transitions, and life's thread being finally cut. Similarly, old colloquialisms for fables, such as spinning a yarn, are reinterpreted by new spin doctors. Spiders' silky threads inspire strong new space fabrics and we weave communications via the worldwide web.

In the seventeenth century architecture dominated exterior design. Landscape architecture was often more of an extension of the formal shapes and rhythms of a building's façade than a separate, creative exercise based on appreciating nature. Versailles, in particular, provided a prestigious example of geometric gardening or mathematical subjugation.

Louis XIV (1643–1715) constructed a place where plants were subject to tyrannical rule. The king's garden was a demonstration of power, man's power over nature, royal power over that of lesser mortals. Not many people could afford the creation, or upkeep, of such vast, intricately manicured parterres.

Portions of the army were employed, discreetly, by night to move massive trees into place. Many men and trees died during this insensitive, political process. Engineers were volunteered to divert water, and to force it into extravagant heights, again to prove personal power over nature. As well as seeking the control of natural forces, exotics were imported. The design and complex running of the *Orangerie*, indicated staggering affluence in a cold northern climate. In the freezing winter, plants would be planted out to welcome the king as he entered a building, perish in the cold, to be instantly replaced with fresh greenhouse victims.

The seasons themselves were denied. The Sun King wished to promote the flattering hypothesis that he himself was the source of life, generating light. He reversed the usual seating arrangements in his chapel so that his subjects, backs to the altar, could have the thrill of observing him. The king modestly performed ballets within his park, magnificently attired, dancing the symbolic, life-giving role of the sun. This megalomaniacal attitude to sculpting scenery provides a telling antithesis to subtler approaches. Take the Japanese tradition. Within this, Zen and Tea Masters (sometimes interchangeable) modified nature with different aims, different results, seeking poverty surpassing riches. By trying to flow with the rhythm of natural forms such as natural streams, they were inspired by the opposite end of the creative spectrum. They tried to work with nature and to dissolve egoism.

Bo Jeffares Sekine, Tea House Window

Where Versailles stands for human dictatorship, Japanese tea gardens represent a desire for aesthetic integration. Wanting to detach themselves from material worries, Zen gardeners wished to blend with their natural environments. To an extent they thus anticipated the motivation of modern environmentalists keen to harmonise with existing sites, and to work as sensitively as possible to fit in with natural conditions and species.

Borrowed Vistas

During the Japanese Civil War (1467–1568) when sudden death was the norm, rich powerful merchants (themselves often, ironically, dealing in the arms trade and consequently rewarded with aristocratic privileges) sought solace in Zen gardens and participating in the tea ceremony. This was deemed a quietening ritual designed to make fate seem more palatable.

Before a battle participants might use bamboos and hangings to set up an enclosure to calm their minds with a tea ceremony. In those days the fire, a potent energy symbol, was left burning in a tea master's house, so that this healing ritual could take place at any time. People shared green tea, a bitter medicinal herb, originally imported (like so much of Japanese culture) from China. Like Native Americans sharing peace pipes, the Japanese sought harmony through this stylised communion.

Bo Jeffares Sekine, Noguch's Heaven, Series

Focusing on the ephemeral beauties about them, they felt they could distance and detach themselves from the greed and destruction dominating their human world (including their own actions and obsessions). They focused instead on other kinds of reality, cherishing the inner peace promoted by the interlocking aesthetic of the tea ceremony. Using the modest space of the teahouse and its garden, they aspired to the kind of inner and outer detachment promoted by esoteric Buddhism, becoming nothing, fusing with the void.

The *genus loci*, or spirit of a place, inspires many Zen and tea gardens. Japanese designers are at their most successful cultivating the feeling of an 'unspoilt' location. Disconcertingly 'natural' gardens have a transcendental capacity, like the famous 'thin' places in Celtic myth, where divisions between different realms appear transparent. Japanese landscapers prefer to work with their site rather than against it, editing trivia such as messy undergrowth to emphasise unique features such as dramatic boulders. Rather than formulating abstract plans first, and then imposing them on a particular place, these artists intuitively seek the intrinsic possibilities of each site.

The Japanese have never consciously rejected their early animist or pantheistic native religion, Shinto (are often happy to have it coexist with later religious imports, such as Buddhism or Christianity.) Japan has an innate respect for natural and elemental forces. Mount Fuji is still worshipped. Builders still perform ceremonies to appease earth spirits before laying the foundations for their buildings.

Because there is such a traditional respect for the inter-related elements of nature, Japanese gardeners work to anticipate climatic cycles and seasonal flora. They value the idiosyncrasies of raw materials. Irregular rock formations are prize exhibits, bought and sold, as in China, for their distinctive character. Artificially ornate, complex sentimental statuary (of the kind decorating formal, Western parks and gardens) are rejected for simpler more organic effects.

Just as understated, earth-clad walls of a tea house provide a perfect foil for surrounding foliage, so the whole tea garden provides a showcase for climatic change. Visitors are aware of movements caused by breezes, sounds of birds, gliding fish, scents after rainfall, transience. Harmonising with nature, hardy plants thriving in the wild are cherished for their resilience. Planting plans can be simple. Bamboo and moss, for example, dramatically offset each other's tactile and textural structures. Shiny stems of giant bamboos emerge from soft carpets of velvety moss.

Water is allowed to follow its natural inclination and flow downwards, in cascades, trickles or dry river beds. Flowers are not forced: they bloom at will. Respect for the seasons, as arbiters of change, lies at the heart of Japanese nature appreciation. Life and literature are so closely bound up with the seasons, and their accompanying festivals, that they provide an endless fund of nostalgia and anticipation. The year is emotionally spaced out in terms of the seasons and their associated sentiments.

Echoing nature, and therefore predominantly green, tea gardens reflect Japan's colour progressions. In a land where spring and autumn are balanced joys (and equally popular with honeymooners) fiery, autumnal maples are as admired as tiny, early plum buds, first signs of spring.

Bo Jeffares Sekine, Moon and Waterfall

Cherry and cherry blossom viewing parties become a national (sometimes alcoholic) obsession. Fragile, cherry blossoms were incorporated into the Samurai code: fearless warriors were encouraged to die with the instantaneous grace of cherry flowers falling to the ground. Ze-Ami, an actor interpreting the classical Noh theatre, categorised audience types by comparing them with varied cherry flowers. While elegant single blooms represented Japanese people of integrity, big, blousy ones summed up cruder, insensitive types, or worse still, barbarians.

Japan's spring explosions of clashing pinks and reds, cochineal plum blossoms, scarlet salmon and peach japonicas, walls of shocking or sugar pink camellias and azaleas, are overtaken by a cooler range of blue and lilac plants, wisterias, irises, morning glories, and hydrangeas, antidotes to summer heat. Monochrome contrasts in winter expose garden layouts, reveal shining paths after rain, or outline landscape compositions with snow.

Bo Jeffares Sekine, Fire and Water

Links between man and nature are replicated in the types of materials used to build tea houses and gardens. Buildings merge into their surroundings as rough stones lead up to increasingly polished and cut interior shapes. Similarly rougher outer woodwork gives way to smoother internal surfaces. The aesthetic terms *sabi* and *wabi* sum up a preference for a simple, understated and unpretentious rustic kind of creativity. A western parallel could be drawn with the deliberately restrained *modus vivendi* advocated by St. Francis.

Natural materials (the antithesis of the ostentatious gold leaf embellishing political strongholds) included cheap straw and plentiful bamboo. Straw and branches packed mud clad walls. Rice straw was woven into *tatami* mats underfoot. Rice paper filled the squares of the sliding screens, or *shoji*, to provide soft, gentle light. Versatile bamboo was used in fencing and screening, cut lengthwise to provide drainpipes, or sliced into sections to make minimalist flower vases.

So, while endless time and energy might be devoted to manipulating simple components, such as stones and moss while trying to reach aesthetic perfection, basic structures remained modest. Spaces were created to harmonise human activities, never (in theory) to oppress or dominate them. Spaces were designed on a human scale. One person's space, represented by their sleeping space, or *tatami* mat, became a symbolic building unit.

Most tea houses remained only a few *tatami* mats in size. The wooden building in the first garden designed by a retired seventeenth century Japanese emperor, in his spatial progression of three linked gardens at *Shugaku-in*, was incredibly simple and unpretentious compared with grand landscaping projects like Versailles. A small, enclosed garden is the first stage in a set of unfolding, linked landscapes, including an informal and relaxing walkway through the fields. It concludes with a dramatic scene across Kyoto's encircling mountain ranges. In its furthest distances is a 'borrowed' vista, an aesthetic device for making physically limited spaces appear infinite.

Bo Jeffares Sekine, Bonsai

Fine-tuning man with nature often involves physically slowing him down. The spatial sequences in tea gardens do just that. Collecting outside the garden, politely waiting for their host, guests enter through its gates to walk in single file along its narrow, meandering paths. Deliberately slowed down, their thought patterns become peaceful. The deliberate placing of rough-surfaced, asymmetrical stepping-stones means that no one can rush, or overtake. Consequently each change in the garden's spatial repertoire is appreciated to the full. The host blocks dull paths, making seasonal adjustments, so that his guests appreciate the best of his miniature landscape. Visitors take in the still atmosphere before stopping at a stone container of water, a universal symbol for purification.

The entrance to the tea house, the central space where they will enact the tea ceremony, is often surprisingly small. The physical act of abasement to get through these 'crawling' doors, acts as an instant equaliser – a welcome, if temporary – relaxation in a still predominantly chauvinist and hierarchical society. Within the tea house is another inner recess. Here the *tokonoma* acts as an aesthetic altar displaying the host's cultural theme, as with a minimalist ink painting, set against a single, graceful wild flower.

The placing of pottery (such as the rustic *raku* pottery favoured by tea masters) or the arrangement of food on dishes, like all branches of Japanese aesthetics, involves spatial choices. The Japanese prefer to think in terms of space (and its definition) rather than mass (and its restriction). Their feelings about space are connected to the aesthetic term *ma*, meaning space or pause. This basic principle explains a Japanese love of space, in preference to other elements, an invisible substance or quality caught, or showed up, by material means.

Japanese aesthetics are always more concerned with space, and its definition, than mass, or the accumulation of volume. In their landscaping techniques, physical elements such as trees and rocks are primarily employed to define space. Irregular positioning, like the asymmetrical arrangement of plants and stones, is employed to distil the mind's cares into repose through spatial detachment.

Just as in the West in-spiration suggests drawing in breath or vital energy, so in China *chi* suggests life, as when the body's forces are harmonised by *tai-chi*. Japanese aesthetics show a similar sensitivity. *Ikebana*, for example, or living flower arrangements, incorporates the word *ike* for breath or life. Breath, or air, plays a vital part in any flower arrangement.

A flower arrangement is not seen on its own, but designed for a specific spatial context, such as the framing area of the *tokonoma*. It is traditionally seen within, or with aesthetic reference to, surrounding spaces. An asymmetrical flower arrangement is often contrasted with the formal rectangular backdrop provided by a scroll, or the linked effects of its own shadow.

Everything is a system of checks and balances. In this, martial arts echo the aesthetic arts. Throwing an opponent off balance can allow a lightweight to reverse a powerful attack, outmanoeuvring body bulk with tactical twists, turns and throws. Exercises in asymmetrical, or poetic balance (an antidote to a hierarchical society?) were explored over the centuries in *bonsai*. *Bonsai* are highly pruned dwarf trees or miniature groves starved in small, shallow pots. Bonsai are ever popular in crowded Japanese cities and suburbs, placed by doors on balconies or on rooftop gardens. These deliberately restrained trees are clipped by convention.

It seems significant that the spatial term *fuseki*, originally used in an old text on gardening, to refer to the placing of stepping stones within Japanese gardens, is now used in relation to the pieces used in the game of *go*. This board game, which reflects territorial ambitions, is devoted to outmanoeuvring one's opponent to gain space.

Similarly, the creation of miniature *bonkei*, or tray gardens, allowed people living in crowded conditions to manipulate microcosmic landscapes, and control living elements. The temporary nature of these materials added to their appeal. In the Noh theatre a performance of striking subtlety was praised with the accolade of *hana* – having the temporary bloom, and transitory attraction of an exquisite short-lived flower.

Japanese gardens often contain a hollow bamboo container, which fills with water, and then drops it with a definite, regular splash. This provides a rhythmic pulse as the silence of the garden is paradoxically broken, in order to refocus attention on its tranquillity. Drawing attention to the space between sounds has two functions. These distinctive pauses allow full appreciation of the previous sound, and the last of its vibrations. Such pauses also give space, as in the staged beats or notes of a drummer or *koto* player, for anticipation of the next sound. Thus the use of space, or deliberate pauses, is as fundamental in musical theory and technique as within all the visual arts.

Visually, the minimalist marks of a Zen painter illustrate the same aesthetic principle. They provide the same kind of monitoring system. Sketches highlight the void. Within an ink painting the surface of the paper can represent two or three dimensional space. So within these black and white, often abstract, works there is often no horizon. A deliberate horizon could suggest a deliberate physical limitation, like a shut door, and so evoke a corresponding mental boundary.

Bo Jeffares Sekine, Zen Garden/Celtic Circle

With a Zen painting the viewer's mind with all its unique personal qualities is presented with a creative catalyst, an opportunity to make an imaginative leap into much wider dimensions. Zen landscapes are like the physical landscapes mused on from tea houses; framed by *shoji* screens and dexterous plantings, often with skilful inclusions of an existent vista, or 'borrowed landscape' to further liberate the mind's eye.

Ma is an aesthetic term anticipating modern physics. It can be interchangeably interpreted in terms of either space or time. *Ma* is more concerned with spatial intervals than solid materials. The quality of a teahouse is not so much in its physical structure, its solid walls and roof, as its vacant, enclosed, space, or inner vacuum. This is created, in theory, to detach the mind from everyday reality and move it into more metaphysical realms.

Tea masters often try to transform mundane, or everyday reality by bringing it to the highest possible aesthetic plane. They have conceived the term *mitate* meaning 'borrowed metaphor', 'judging', 're-seeing' or generally revising one's vision. Quantum physics is now being compared with the unifying theories of flux and interplay underlying native cultures. Some Eastern beliefs in a continuous, cyclical time-scale lend creative possibilities to reductionist, separatist, analytical Western thought processes.

The concept of tragedy, for example, can be surprisingly different in Eastern and Western thinking. Within the Western tradition, as established by the ancient Greeks, a tragic situation is one which cannot be put right. A negative situation becomes irrevocable. A death, or deaths, occur. That's it. Final.

Compare the format of a Noh play. Within this Japanese classical tradition, the death or deaths precede the so-called 'action'. Here, the situation is not irrevocable. Indeed the interest lies in the manner of righting wrongs, or trying to restore harmonies. Time is not abruptly sectioned into past, present and future, but is flexible. As in the Aboriginal concept of Dream Time, a continuous yet mythical present unites all aspects of reality. Noh plays include linked dream sequences. In these 'dream' episodes barriers between earthly time, space and gravity dissolve. Dreams like these allow for easy communication between different beings, including humans, ghosts and gods.

The power of thought is shown to be forceful on any level. Compassion promotes prayer to dissolve obsessive hatreds, and destructive negative emotions which block peaceful evolution. Complete harmony is, according to Zen practitioners, a state of nothingness. For them, nothingness means everything. This is a

Bo Jeffares Sekine, Universe/Black Mandala

paradox. By losing one's egocentric nature, becoming nothing, one harmonises with the cosmos. Compare this kind of 'positive' negativity or absence of discord, with the mathematical concept of zero, a useful logical concept of spatial negation.

The concept of the 'vanishing point' which emerged in Renaissance Europe from the interactions of artists, architects and mathematicians, was crucial to their attempts to clearly depict a three dimensional world in two dimensions. The 'vanishing point' logically pins an image in space. In Eastern thinking there can be more of an intuitive synthesis, ideally the

172 | Creativity Nature and Us

moment when the viewer's mind becomes free to merge with the absolute. This kind of integration, where physical space becomes a metaphor for infinite space, assumes a measure of acceptance. And acceptance, in the spiritual sense, implies an awareness of the positive potential in everything and everyone.

St. Francis chose to meditate in a four foot cube. This conscious, spatial limitation inspired the modern sculptor Antony Gormley. He has worked with Chinese Zen monks from the Shaolin temple, a birthplace of oriental martial arts. When creating a stage set for an international tour he just used boxes. These minimal spaces became flexible assets. The monks use the life size boxes to sum up frustrations in a dramatic dance routine. Gormley felt that we should first recognise our limitations and then 'escape or transcend them'. Thus *Sutra* (2008) is a dramatic comment on how anyone can feel 'boxed in'. Boxes can be beds, shelves, baths, tables, boats or tombs. You can be in, on, or by them in any number of ways but, as he points out, 'you occupy them mentally by how you think of them': Imagination, as always, inspires vision. Creativity allows us to transcend our limitations and literally think 'outside the box'.

Why do people increasingly say they 'need space'? They equate 'personal space' with the freedom to relax, to be themselves. They may equally imply they need peace to meditate on their problems. Healers suggest creative visualisations to conjure up perfect places. This calms the mind, allowing dream dramas to work themselves out unconsciously resolving challenges and solving conflicts. While we sleep psychic spring cleaning systems seem to be on automatic.

Dreams seem as mysterious in human terms as nebulous cloud formations in the sky. In dreams, or imaginative reverie, landscaping projects have no spatial limits. Unhindered by temporal, monetary or gravitational limitations we create with our subconscious minds. We translate emotions directly into metaphysical imagery. We make movies. We direct, produce, act and perform our own special effects.

Envisaging Reality

Sight and vision are synonymous with our attitudes to life. If we say that someone sees things in perspective, we imply a sense of relative order or sensible priorities. And, whenever we see 'eye to eye', we are happy to be in complete agreement.

Eyesight (such as El Greco's presumed astigmatism and peculiar visions, or the ageing Corot's transition from cool classicism to later blurred, soft-focus romanticism) is said to reflect personality. So too does tunnel vision. The phrase 'short sighted' is synonymous with mental limitation, and a 'closed' mind. Farsightedness is equated with emotional range and anticipation and the pleasant spatial concept of an 'open' mind.

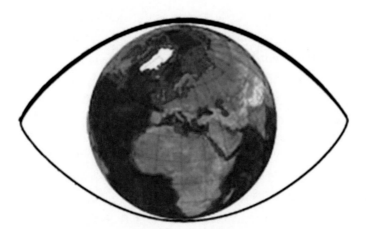

Bo Jeffares Sekine, Sky Eye

Someone mentally limited, without clear vision, cannot see the wood for the trees. Ideally, we see the whole as well as its composite parts. Thus the 'London Eye', and others like it, are so called because they allow people to see further. Native Americans, scanning the distant horizon for friends or foes, consciously switched from near to far focus, to retain maximum mental as well as visual flexibility. Similarly, some governments try to train individuals with intuitive powers as psychic investigators. Such people are then symbolically described as 'far' or 'distant' viewers.

Paul Klee, famous for declaring that art 'renders visible' also coined the perceptive phrase the 'Thinking Eye'. We program our minds to edit and select. Invisible preconceptions determine what we see and consequently register. The symbol of an open eye was selected for the United States of America's Great Seal and printed on her bank notes.

Romantics see the eye as the 'window of the soul'. Psychics refer to the third eye (or pineal gland) as the site for Extra Sensory Perception. Our visual range depends on the scale of our core beliefs, or current paradigm. Tests prove that even complete illiterates instinctively recognise key concepts, such as vital words for 'Police' or 'Whisky'.

Varying angles of perception can add to our psychological scope – hence the invention of cubism, a flat play with angles, to suggest three dimensional images. Zen monks equate peace of mind with the reflection of the moon on still water. The sun's light illuminates the moon. The moon's reflected light is then further distilled, as it is reflected onto still water. Adapted verbally or visually, this theme enhances reflection.

Bo Jeffares Sekine, Moon Reflected on Still Water

Artists and writers traditionally provide new reflections of reality to illuminate the processes of life. Mirrors also reflect these activities, as when Velazquez relegated his king and queen to a distant reflection, reversing the accepted social order. Magritte, playing with perception, a word which combines both physically looking and psychologically understanding, decided to place a cloudscape within an eye. He provocatively entitled his image *Le Faux Mirroir* (1929).

Man-made mirrors circulate in space. Information from these man-made eyes, like the Hubble space telescope's 'ultra deep field' photographs, can illustrate tantalising reflections of our universe light-years ago.

Time and space, once considered separate, become harder to unravel – like Martin Luther King's picture of the composite human race as a single, interwoven 'garment'.

Now is the only reality: time and space the warp and weft of our lives blend together as an integrated or seamless fabric. Varieties of time, past and the future, go out of fashion. Einstein stated that distinctions between past, present and future are only a 'persistent illusion'.

While the present appears omnipotent, subjective evaluations of it seem endless. The reflective time which would have been poured into the concentrated production and perusal of hand painted *Books of Hours* in Mediaeval times, for example, is hard to grasp in an age characterised by technical transmissions. Meditative reflection seems to be superceeded by mechanical virtuosity.

Communication was once such a laborious process. Imagine slowly inscribing wet clay tablets, marking bark or papyrus rolls or carefully incising shapes onto hard stone tablets. The news was a product of scribes, singers, poets, fast riders and energetic gossips. Events can now be photographed and filmed as they occur. Space satellites relay ideas and actions instantaneously. We experience synchronicity.

Diderot, helping to popularise some of the democratic ideals underlying the French Revolution, played his part by helping to make current knowledge common currency. The publication of his vast encyclopaedias, the opening of public libraries, the transfer of knowledge via the media and computer networks have all added to our independence.

Thought-wise, people tended to be kept on a fairly strict subsistence diet, or a set menu. We live in a self-service era. People like to pick and choose. We increasingly question imposed hereditary, social and cultural programs. We attempt to review and restructure our negative and outdated beliefs. We try to free our minds.

Magic and Miracles

The old idea of magic is still apposite. It suggests ways in which people can visualise beliefs. Cavemen used it, as a psychological rehearsal, to better understand their prey and catch it. They magically depicted scenes of successful hunts, as a subconscious means of helping them happen. Even Picasso, a supposedly 'modern' creator, believed in the power of thought to activate events, make things come true. We play with magic all the time. When we say 'picture this' or 'imagine that' we start to fabricate the future.

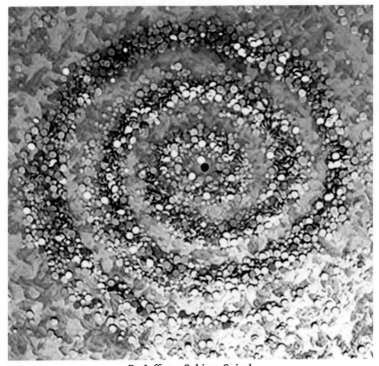

Bo Jeffares Sekine, Spiral

Define a miracle? Attempting to define the impossible, or the invisible, the human mind gets tricky. Because it does not like to accept limitations, its instinct is to push existing boundaries. The human imagination continually seeks new ways of problem solving. We try to make the impossible start to become possible, then probable, then actual. Some people tease scientists saying that miracles are merely part of a much larger reality which they have not yet understood, catalogued, taken credit for, or marketed.

Take time travel, frequently discussed by spiritual guides and science fiction authors, for whom gravity is never a problem. Advanced astral travel could certainly cut down on holiday costs. Travellers from other realms, sometimes viewed as angelic messengers, bringers of hope and healing (whose wings symbolise an ability to move between all kinds of dimensions) are reinterpreted in each era.

Do we have visitors from outer space, extra terrestrials, currently investigating us just as Shakespeare's actors examined the native inhabitants of their exotic island? Because beliefs create reality, people are ever tuned into their own expectations of what is currently 'real' for them. Subconsciously we define the parameters of what is true for us, defining or restricting all possibilities, whether they are visible or invisible.

How do you show invisible factors? Two people from contrasting times and backgrounds illustrate that it is possible to make the unbelievable credible, the invisible visible. Piero della Francesca's *Resurrection* (c.1452) and Raoul Dufy's *La Fée Eléctricite* (1937) both deal with mysterious energies and try to transmit optimism. Piero is formal, Dufy frivolous. Where Piero crystallises, Dufy fantasises. Piero was interested in the music of the spheres and pure mathematics. Dufy enjoyed popular music broadcast on that new invention the 'wireless,' some electrical contraption for communicating with the masses.

Piero's image exploits time and colour to create serenity. Without a hint of sentimentality, he presents a clear picture of Christ riding a cloud after rising from the dead, his pink robe echoing the faint pink light of dawn, indicating a new awakening within a continuous life.

Dufy evokes the gods of Greek legend to suggest creative continuity. He portrays a modern subject. He depicts the spirit of electricity, an energy goddess for our times. The Greeks' absorption in energy interchanges and philosophical curiosity about intangibles make them our intellectual precursors. Their mythical deities are combined in Dufy's composite creation. It mixes scientists and musicians. Why? Dufy decided to make invisible electricity seem 'real,' and so fashioned a poetic metaphor to capture its essence. He doesn't depict a pop up toaster or a massive power station, but a more intangible delight – music – the traditional 'food of love'.

By suggesting the recording and broadcasting of invisible sound waves passing through the ether, he evokes universal aspects of electricity. He portrays it as a potential source of joy and harmony. He includes the cinema or *théâtre électrique* in a vast panorama in praise of democratic pleasures.

Dufy's allegorical method, his update of classical themes within a dramatic contemporary context, links him with other great, creative masters including Shakespeare. Dufy's selection of lightning flashes for his central image, flanked by cloud-formed figures, gods and turbines, parallels Shakespeare's melding of magic and mortals in *The Tempest*. The painter's thunder and lightning parallel the dramatist's use of tempestuous imagery. Both artists direct our attention to the interplay of eternal energies. Their dramas indicate tensions building up before, and then peace being restored as violent storms subside.

An artist's value lies in the degree to which they absorb the lessons of the past and make them their own. Dufy speaks with a deceptively relaxed, spontaneous voice. He interweaves colours, symbols and emotions. He devised his own battery of technical tricks, utilising them to express an effervescent vision of universal interactions.

He achieves this with a deceptively simple, childlike style. Seemingly casual patches of colour are covered with sketchy, decorative designs. This style loosely unifies his upbeat compositions. Figures from the mythical past and popular present co-exist (as they do in *The Fable of Arachne*). Science is made palatable. His parable praises invisible forces' abilities to enrich our everyday existence, to make life fun.

Many miracles evoke light. Light is a real and a symbolic quality. The word light evokes luminosity, the antidote to dullness. Light suggests radiance and a lack of worldly, or material, gravitas. Lighten up means cheer up. Light suggests intellectual clarity (as in the term Enlightenment) as well as optimistic love. It also encapsulates spirituality as in the statement: 'I am the light'.

Recording near-death experiences (as when their hearts may have temporarily stopped but their consciousness has somehow continued) people often record moving into bright, shadowless light. Artists experiment with light sources such as fire light, sunlight, moonlight and starlight. Successful people are called 'stars'.

Light and colour merge in rainbows, luminous sky symbols. Coming after thunderous storms they signify peace. Ovid evokes one in *Metamorphoses*, Shakespeare personifies one as the heavenly messenger concluding *The Tempest*. Queen Elizabeth I was painted holding a rainbow a reminder of biblical references to positive connections with God. A rainbow represents a divine pact with man as light bridges heaven above and earth below.

Rubens places a rainbow in a painting of his final home. Millais places two, touchingly, behind his famous portrait of *The Blind Girl* (1856). Hiroshige, in *Ushimachi, near the Takanawa Gate* (1857) reveals himself as a master of geometric parallels. He links the mundane and the marvellous. He places the curve of a rainbow high in the sky above the repeated curve of two melon rinds. His transient curve of light links with the fruit, bitten back to curved lines of pink, white and green, lying down in the street below.

Powerful lines of colour, as in a striped deck chair, present Jim Dine's interpretation of a rainbow, a panel in his powerful *Studio Landscape* of 1963. And the Australian artist, Sidney Nolan, experiments with the Aboriginals' metaphysical concept of the Rainbow Serpent.

The fact that rainbow colours can be seen as separate, yet are harmoniously fused, inspires themes of separate yet co-existent levels of reality. Just as light was traditionally shown emanating from saints' heads, so healers and increasing numbers of scientists suggest that all of our bodies emit subtle, fluctuating waves or vibrations, which can be translated as spiritual auras, or practically labelled as surrounding energy fields.

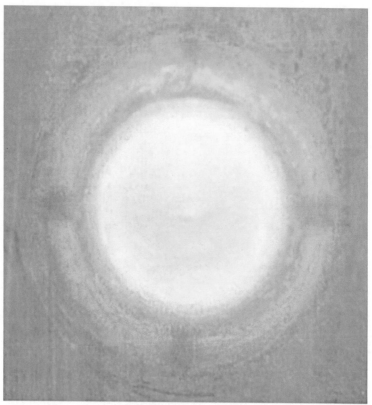

Bo Jeffares Sekine, Light

Red represents an energetic, earthy attitude. Each colour has its own attributes. Pink suggests sensitivity, turquoise creativity, purple power, and white containing all the colours personifies purity and attainment. As we evolve and hopefully become more content our auras become correspondingly brighter and clearer. But inconsistencies also add variety and richness to life. Shelley summed this up, praising individual flaws, or failings, which act like prisms or stained glass to tint the white radiance of eternity.

Bo Jeffares Sekine, DNA Landscape

How can artists portray astronauts weightless in space? Compositions without formal backgrounds, like those depicting figures in water, provide parallels. Look at Breughel's hubraic depiction of *The Fall of Icarus* (1558?), a pair of legs discreetly disappearing into a calm ocean. Popular beach holidays and pools have led to more disjointed or floating bodies, by artists such as R.B. Kitaj. Exotic water paintings include Gauguin's Pacific idylls. One of his images of figures in a landscape setting, painted in 1878, has as its title the kind of perennial questions children are always asking adults (and adults secretly ask themselves) *'Where do we come from?' 'Who are we?' 'Where are we going?'*

Life Paths

Gauguin's own voyages from his native Denmark to Paris and then to the South Seas were, like those of the tubercular Scot, Robert Louis Stevenson, fuelled by romantic escapism. Artistic migrations, usually from north to south, help us chart their motivation. Fearing war, and extermination, many European artists fled fascism. Seen as dangerous undesirables and troublemakers, their mass exodus moved modern art from France to America. This drift continues as artists are drawn to America's popular culture.

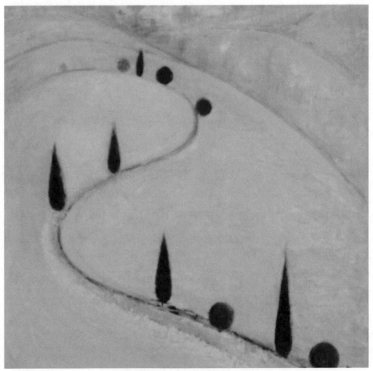

Bo Jeffares Sekine, Road of Life

David Hockney was raised in the north of England, trained in London, and then emigrated to California's sunnier scenery. Celebrating his relaxed lifestyle, he painted *Mulholland Drive: The Road to the Studio* (1980). This twenty foot canvas encapsulates a personal journey, symbolically choreographing his motoring experience, mapping familiar landmarks on a winding route from the Hollywood hills to his new, creative base.

This road picture eschews traditional perspective, of the kind evoked in a later photo-collage, a more realistic image of *Pearblossom Hwy, 11–18 April, no. 2* (1986). The latter is an empty, sign and litter-lined highway, stretching out into the spatial distance. An all-encompassing, technological adaptation of the road of life is reflected in the invisible realms of 'information highways'.

A journey of life remains an archetypal preoccupation. We seek inner freedom, matched by outer adventure. This is illustrated by endless images of roads, paths and rivers. From egg to embryo, baby to child, teenager to adult, elder of excellence (or person in their second childhood) to compost (and/or ethereal being) change is the norm.

Metamorphosis was summed up microcosmically by insects such as butterflies. Able to adapt to different elements, butterflies evolve from earth-loving worms, via cocoons, to a flying species complete with altered DNA. Dragonflies go one further. These insects move from earth to water to air. Born in the mud at the bottom of a pond, they crawl up suitable plant stalks to emerge onto dry surfaces, dry out and fly off.

Our own mythical adventures follow similar patterns, plus a few extra trials and tribulations along the way. These frequently include spiritual journeys progressing from low lands to higher ranges. (Capricorns are designed to evolve from materialistic, mud-loving crocodiles to independent, free-spirited mountain goats). On any journey like attracts like. Outer reality reflects inner consciousness. This inner journey, according to Yeats, is the only journey.

Archetypal beliefs are packed with exploratory themes and related landscape challenges. Richard Long climbs to isolated peaks as part of his life's journey. He is described by his friend Carl Andre as a 'backpacker'. Long describes his art, or walking experiences, as realistic. He states he is a Realist dealing with 'real stones, real time, real actions'. He denies being an illusionist or a conceptualist. Yet there is a symbolic element to his work, and also a metaphysical one. Look how early on, in 1969, he distinctly subtitled a record of a walking tour in Germany *'When Attitudes Become Form'*. Long illustrates how minds mould matter. He admits that a walk usually 'demonstrates or carries out an idea'. So, for all his talk of just placing natural finds – 'raw materials' such as sticks and stones – he is actually thought motivated.

Early dust and ash lines evolve. Influenced by the musician John Cage's view of the whole world as a work of art, Long's art adapts maps, recalls sounds, and includes the kindness of strangers. His walks also refer to history and science. He chose to walk, for example, from an early Neolithic to an early industrial site in Britain to suggest England's shift from basic agriculture to mechanised productivity. Similarly, in 2008, he decided to walk from ancient stone structures in Carnac in Brittany (perhaps set up as early stellar observatories) to Cerne, in Switzerland, currently renowned for its oval particle accelerator. This symbolic journey from past to present was entitled *Megalithic to Subatomic*.

Moving along ancient Nazca lines, in Peru, where giant forms, such as a vast spider, can only be properly viewed from high above, Long saw himself in the tradition of earlier earth artists, many of whom seemed deeply conscious of what was happening in the skies above them. *Walking to a Solar Eclipse* in 1999 he used a personal journey to try to link microcosmic and macrocosmic forces.

The Garden of Cosmic Speculation, with its comet bridge, makes astronomical facts more tangible. Jencks develops solid symbols for scientific theories about the way we view space. An energy explosion, matter turning into energy, is portrayed in metal from a photograph taken within the 'cloud chamber' of a nuclear accelerator. This elegant three dimensional sculptural composition, with its reflection in still water, gracefully sums up a sub-atomic explosion.

Microcosms and macrocosms link what happens within our bodies, on the earth and also in outer space. Jencks is flexible: he considers changing models of the universe. He also attempts a model of the whole evolutionary process. His *Universe Cascade* is inspirational. What would you decide on? Would you include sex and consciousness? What blend of art and science, site and scale, matter and focus would you use to express your own unique vision? For his experiment he chose a descending pattern. The antithesis of ambitious triangular and prism shaped pyramids designed to reach up to the skies, his flowing cascade focused not on a man-made concepts of perfection but on nature herself.

Jencks saw evolution as a staged process so he made a correspondingly staged structure. He thinks evolution jumps, at key points, as in human development and learning processes, to trigger new growth patterns. So he systematically staggered the descent of his water flow, cascading down from his house into a lake below. Stones, collected with his daughter from nearby riverbanks, are incorporated into the grand design, along with imported Chinese rocks, like great stone clouds. Fossils and mosaics form simple shapes, symbolic circles. The whole invites speculation about how we could tackle our future.

At some point in the distant future our sun is going to explode. Our galaxy is going to collide with another, larger one. These are facts. Alterations in our life-support system, the sun (and the consequent heat and light we receive) may tempt scientists to try and harness passing asteroids or employ other techniques still incubating in the realms of science fiction. The connection of cosmic spirals due in three billion years time, when the Andromeda Galaxy bumps into ours, provides food for thought. We may be sucked into a black hole, or spun out into distant space. It will no longer be a case of adapting the home environment, but inventing a new scenario – leaving the Earth perhaps, moving to a new planet, adapting completely new spatial scenery?

Posing fundamental questions, Jencks takes over a niche previously occupied by saints and sages. What is reality? What is the future of mankind? The architect forges metaphysical symbols to elucidate mysteries. He becomes an educator. Avoiding a political or sectarian bias, he implies a spiritual perspective by focusing his attention – and ours – on eternal change.

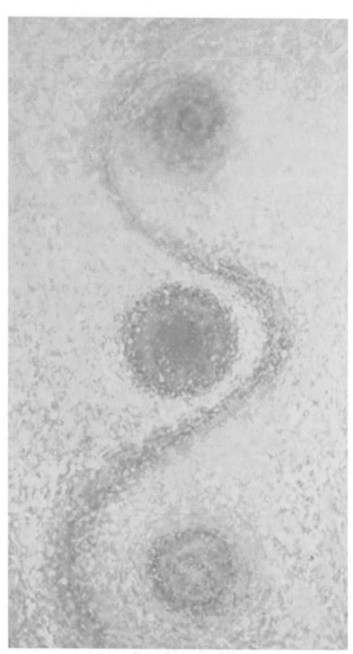

Bo Jeffares Sekine, Evolution

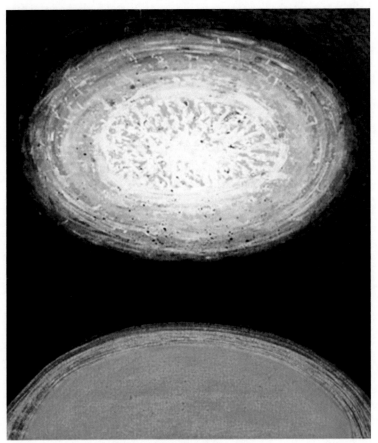

Bo Jeffares Sekine, Earth and Space

Personal evolution can be depicted as a journey along a particular route. Dangerous scenic qualities are equated with facing life-threatening dangers, or the thrill of gaining spectacular prizes. People enact quests, exercise free will or evoke guidance within these karmic frameworks fleshed out by standard metaphysical props. In *The Pilgrim's Progress*, for example, written by Bunyan in 1678, the fictional format reflects the author's own puritanical mindscape. Specific areas which the pilgrim moves through reflect corresponding stages in his emotional development, such as the gloomy Slough of Despond. This whole tale presents a moral testing ground.

Gardens provide miniature versions of symbolic terrains. Shusaku Arakawa and American writer and artist Madeline Gris challenged the traditional concept of the peaceful Japanese stroll garden, turning it on its head. Earlier land artists in Japan sought unobtrusive materials to discreetly blend in with natural effects. They created delicate visual sequences blending into distant landscape features such as the Kyoto hills. Framing spatial progressions provided a way to stretch visitors' imaginative responses. Wandering down elegant, meandering pathways made them relaxed and calm.

Innovative creators, these two employed shock tactics. They created a surrealist mix of living plants, odd architectural and domestic items. Presented with a set of *Directions of Use* on entering this *Site of Reversible Destinies* (1995), people encounter disorientation. There are roof tiles on the ground, strange staircases, peculiar paths, abrupt awkward angles and half-sunk kitchen units. Spatial incongruities destabilise. This was a conscious upheaval of centuries of concentrated effort seeking painstaking perfection and subtle sophistication. *The Site* of *Reversible Destinies* attacks established cultural norms to provoke new perceptions of life.

Each civilization creates its own arenas for change. Homer conceived the archetypal hero Ulysses who travelled the wine-dark seas being tested by a set of mythical adventures. Just as this classical hero met monsters and was tempted by the sirens, so in *Tom Jones* (1749), Fielding's mock epic, his comic hero enjoyed sexual encounters gained on picaresque travels through the English countryside as a part of an educational journey. James Joyce also reinterprets the Ulysses myth, as a middle-aged businessman experiences a sleazy day in contemporary Dublin. The artist De Chirico' provides ironic suburban parables, like the popular cartoon character 'Homer' Simpson.

Nadine Gordimer parodies the theme of a successful journey representing a successful life, or set of aspirations, with grim restraint in the undignified death of *A Guest of Honour* (1970). Her hero's corpse is unceremoniously dumped on an anonymous dirt track in a country he had once rushed to help. The reversal, a triumphal road of life theme, is expressed by Nelson Mandela in (1995) in his inspirational, autobiographical story *A Long Walk to Freedom*.

Moving from individuals to groups, politicians projecting plans refer to them as 'road maps'. Moving from the mystic to the mechanical, traditional agrarian sites metamorphose into utilitarian equivalents. Thus in the public imagination the sacred groves and graceful nymphs decorating classical art are replaced by plastic theme parks. Arcadia, a word for paradise, adorns shopping arcades. Romantic outdoor picnics, immortalised by Watteau and the Impressionists, are replaced by images of identikit bean tins symptomatic of instant, standardised meals cloned by useful plastic food chains and processed in efficient, impersonal service stations.

Compare our attitude to cars with our traditional respect for horses, our former major means of transport. Cared for and cherished, they are recorded with honour in so many ancient stories and corresponding artworks. These records can be as varied as miniature Etruscan statuettes, or early examples of earth art, vast, white horses scratched out on England's chalky downs. Horses lent prestige to warriors and leaders alike. Velasquez produced power portraits of kings and conquerors, deftly angling our eyes up towards idealised figures depicted high up on their elegant prancing steeds. Horses could also provide companionship for travel or repetitive agrarian tasks. Constable included sturdy farm horses as an integral and reassuring part of his rustic harmonies.

René Magritte, Le Thérapeute

Cars are faster. While glamorous cars, like gas-guzzling planes, may act as the ultimate fashion accessory for film and pop stars, they burn oil and emit toxic fumes poisoning our planet. So we entertain mixed feelings about them. Compare, say, the realistic reverence of a horse portrait by Stubbs, in the eighteenth century, with a squashed metal cube, expendable junk, by Claes Oldenburg in the twentieth century, equating cars with scrap.

Travellers in literature, like figures in landscapes, become less essential. The landscape itself, a sense of a empty, wild, natural expanse can capture our imaginations. *Wuthering Heights* (1847) could not exist without its wide, atmospheric moor or be emotionally recast within a village shop or concrete tower block. This untamed, windswept moorland creates an elemental mood, atmospherically colouring the entire novel. The more cluttered the world gets, the more people crave physical space, the more desperate they become for escapist images of such uncontaminated open panoramas.

Magritte's space games are unique. Putting captions and contents at odds, he provokes speculation. His image of a therapist in *Le Thérapeute*, (1937), shows a figure stuffed with clouds. Is his message: Healer heal yourself?

Similarly, *Les Mémoires d'un Saint* (1966) is a bland painting of empty space with an apparently nostalgic title. This title in the hands of an arch romantic, such as Caspar David Friedrich a century earlier, would have reinforced a sentimental link between man and nature. Magritte is more existential. This is one of his most restrained pictures. It is also one of his most memorable. Suggesting an empty stage, a scroll almost fills his neutral canvas. There is no specific floor or horizon line. Its incurved ends suggest theatrical curtains. Imagine a floating still from a lost film, an unnerving, detached backdrop from some uneventful life.

This suspended image, itself in an empty space, depicts another empty space merging sea and sky. These are depicted in similar pale blues. White wave and cloud formations fuse along the horizon. This standardised effect is so impersonal it seems sterile. The overall effect is the very opposite of Velazquez's curtained experiment with spatial progression in *The Fable of Arachne* : the inner heart of this painterly image is executed with verve and gusto. Does Magritte's title *Les Mémoires d'un Saint* suggest a saint, untainted by worldly concerns, at one with the elements, or so neutral as to be nonexistent? Magritte may be presenting us with a paradox (like a Zen *ko-an*) designed to provoke curiosity.

Les Mémoires d'un Saint falls into the category of delayed shock. No baroque exuberance, no schoolboy humour, no Daliesque absurdities, just a quiet displacement of everyday reality.

Magritte's metaphysical wit upended traditional symbols, and made perplexing use of our standard vocabulary. Magritte juggled with what was traditionally inside and outside the picture frame. His games with eyes and windows stimulate emotional revisions. He implicitly questioned all the rules of the game relating to orthodox views on time, sex and gravity. His works – painted, photographed, cast in bronze, or combined in collages – combine verbal and visual ironies. Disquieting statements (such as those uttered by Shakespeare's wise fools) provoke a questioning approach.

Magritte makes us question traditional concepts of time and space. Perhaps he is anticipating experiments in virtual reality?

Can this intuitive imagery provide parallels with scientific formulae to explain relativity? Einstein's equation may be logical, but Magritte makes us ponder, poetically, on the continuous interplay of facts and feelings.

Inspired by dream sequences, Magritte made his dead pan images all the more compelling by representing them in an apparently 'realistic' format. Smooth surfaces seem 'real.' They are painstakingly exact. Apparently natural effects, bordering at times on photo-realism, lend credibility to ambiguous compositions.

Bo Jeffares Sekine, River

Thus in *Les Mémoires d'un Saint* the representational exactitude of the 'material' painted on the curtain side of the painted scroll, and the authenticity of all his standardised waves and clouds, help weld this hybrid presentation together. Where Velasquez could work up vibrant colour sequences, contrasting thick impasto with textured strokes and delicate touches, Magritte's blue-grey palette was essentially lifeless, and his technique mechanical. There is a cold synthesis of impersonal artifice and timeless space in this immense dissolving ocean.

Water is also adapted to show personal progress, as on symbolic river journeys. Starting from fresh springs and gradually progressing towards the sea, rivers provide continuous background flow. They can help to match physical exploration with mental maturity: the fact that Mark Twain's young hero Tom Sawyer in *The Adventures of Huckleberry Finn* (1884), grows up on the banks of the Mississippi, and has formative adventures there, puts his adolescence into a rich, worldly context. Tom's evolution takes place against the backdrop of a busy waterway, complete with travellers, traffic and implications of much wider horizons as this river flows to meet the ocean.

The ancient Greeks saw the crossing of the River Styx as a symbolical allegory for moving from one reality to another. Our archetypal term the River of Life has a literary echo in the term 'stream of consciousness.' A stream of consciousness novel allows one idea or feeling to flow imperceptibly into the next. Time and space become fluid echoing the title of one of Chagall's works from 1939 – *Time is a River without Banks*.

Clouds

Within the vast range of our landscape vocabulary, clouds probably represent our most mysterious and adaptive image for transience. Anthony Gormley's *Quantum Cloud* (2000) defined a human body space with surrounding metal rods. And a temporary creation called *Blind Light* (2007) deliberately disorientated people as they tried to negotiate thick, noise-dampening fog. Central to this interactive piece, was the spatially confused public's emotional ambiguity as they tried to feel their way through soft, featureless mist.

Bo Jeffares Sekine, Pink Cloud

Where rock is associated with durability, 'diamonds are a girl's best friend', clouds signal change. Magritte, consciously reversing the norm as usual, filled his skies with floating rocks. Where stone is chosen to try to materialise permanent legacies, cloud comes into its own as a medium for imaginative speculation, as in *Antony and Cleopatra* (1623):

> 'Sometimes we see a cloud that's dragonish;
> A vapour sometime like a bear or lion.'

Because they are by nature chameleon-like, clouds lend themselves to comparisons with related patterns in nature. Look at Gerald Manley Hopkins' well-known comparison of cloud formations with patterns on fish, his famous 'mackerel skies'. The poet developed his theory of 'inscape,' as opposed to landscape, as miniature blueprints draw our attention to the way in which minute examples of natural design provide microscopic keys to other materialisations. His poetic concept of inscape anticipates modern links between minute nanotechnologies and boundless cosmology.

Noguchi's *Sky Gate* focused our attention up into the heavens through a solid stone gateway. Another sculptor, Anish Kapoor plays with the void by adapting reflected surfaces. In busy Chicago he made a huge rounded form called *Cloud Gate* in 2004. Mirroring both passing clouds and passers-by this convex construction bends all images. As ever, reflections of individuals like ants moving over an egg are interpreted according to each person's physical eyesight and their own interpretations of existence.

Reversed viewers are seen upside down in the reflective surface of another huge wave-like structure. 'Sky Mirror' was created in

2001 in Nottingham, Britain. It is gently concave. This distorts its reflective properties – so realities are subtly altered. Reverse psychology can make us reconsider spatial values.

Kapoor's *Sky Mirror* in New York (2006), reverses the city's sky scrapers to capture soft, tinted clouds passing within its concave dish. It distorts time and space. In this built-up site, even a glimpse of open sky is refreshing. It is a refreshing antidote to so many hard, geometric buildings blocking out crucial sunlight. Kapoor designed this *Sky Mirror* to 'bring the sky down to ground'. Earth and sky should be complementary.

An early fractal was named the orchid fractal, because of its resemblance to this plant form. Similar links exist between natural phenomena and abstract mathematics. The ratios of massed lines or bountiful dots decorating the bodies of fish and animals appear to follow hidden rules. Thus the ironically named Chaos Theory reveals insights into how an apparently random universe obeys its own abstract guidelines. Even the movements of football crowds milling about in vast arenas can be anticipated. The Lorenz attractor allows digital cameras to feed into a pre-programmed computer, which can then direct attention to possible dangers from congestion, as people unconsciously unite to form waves of massed energy.

Energy flows are reflected in wind shaped cloud formations. Clouds remain versatile. Aristophanes adapted them as a comic chorus. Shelley selected them as the essence of change, or flux, within nature in his poem 'Mutability', where he compared us with clouds veiling the midnight moon:

> How restlessly they speed, and gleam, and quiver,
> Streaking the darkness radiantly!

Cloud formations provide landscape links. We look up to see our local clouds. We follow overall weather pictures of the cloud formations encircling our globe as wind, water and temperature interact. Heat causes water vapour to rise up into the air to create more clouds which, as they condense, fall again as rain, or acid rain. Man-made poison clouds move freely, as pollution shows no respect for national boundaries.

Communal cloud effects, like those we study on nearby planets, link us with nebulous masses rearranging themselves on a galactic scale, as chemical particles interact with primary gases. Clouds provide perfect symbols of change. Clouds forming and dispersing illustrate an endless scientific cycle of change both on earth and in outer space. Specific forms, such as a particular cloud, remain unique, individual expressions of the transience of life whilst remaining part of a much wider universal system.

Abstract cycles of transition, each provoking the next, were recognised by Taoism, a Chinese philosophical expression for the constant ebb and flow of all life forces. Taoism clarifies transitions between physical and metaphysical realities. It teaches us to become aware of ideal times to be creative or receptive, defining perfect times for intuitive meditation balanced by those for practical action. Similarly, the term 'cash flow' symbolises a fluid exchange of material assets within an 'economic climate'.

When entrepreneur and philanthropist Bill Gates first heard of the Internet he thought its impact would be like a 'tidal wave'. Now we 'surf the net'. This composite image reworks two traditional symbols for energy and creativity, binding together images of webs and waves. Equally the harmonious phrase 'going with the flow' suggests being in tune with nature, becoming part of the 'bigger picture', being more aware of eternal rhythms, less obsessed with 'small minded' or egotistical priorities.

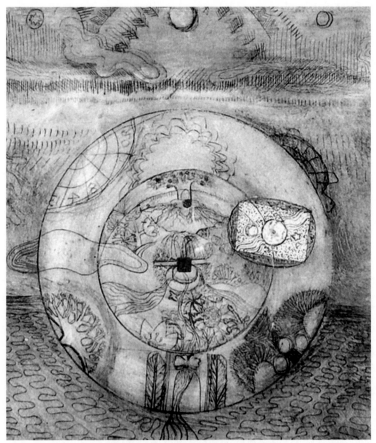

Bo Jeffares Sekine, World and Waves

Earth bound computers utilise spatial technology. Information is broken down into invisible patterns and wavelengths. Unseen messages are transmitted to and fro between satellites high up above our earthly atmosphere. What is there in our traditional vocabulary for skyscapes to describe such transient, amorphous connections and webs? Now bright sparks concoct virtual realities. Their inventions, which combine possible, probable and virtual realms, interact with old realities, now traditionally referred to as The Real World. Hybrid mindsets in cyberspace create a new *zeitgeist*.

Language reflects change. More earthbound in the past, we would traditionally refer to a sensible thinker as someone 'with their feet on the ground'. We would praise a 'rock solid' or dependable personality or situation. Common sense was equated with 'down to earth' values. Now boundaries dissolve. Personal and private data can be accessed via 'windows without walls'. 'Futures' rather than facts fuel our stock markets. One can be divorced for a 'virtual' affair, enacted between invented 'avatars' on the web. Are we morally as well as technically becoming less grounded? As our hearts and minds interact with technology we now casually refer to stored information as being 'in the cloud'.

Turner evoked transparent light-saturated clouds form able to form and dissolve in earthly space. His images of tinted vapour anticipate photographs of immense, coloured nebulas sent back to us by the Hubble telescope from outer space. Our world's changes, like her clouds reforming within her atmosphere, echo those of larger, fluctuating galaxies.

Primary gases assemble as huge clouds to form solid stars and planets or transiently deconstruct into the void to create antimatter or negative space. This nebulous alteration between solid and invisible states has its parallels in our animistic and spiritual beliefs.

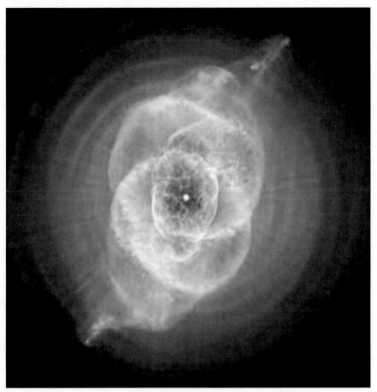

The Cat's Eye Nebula

For many cultures life and death, like day and night, were complementary states of being. Being born and dying (rites of passage) were just phases of transition; entry and exit points to a specific stage, our Earth. This approach, concentrating less on objects and more on stages of becoming, has parallels in modern scientific thought. Reductionist focus is replaced with growing appreciation of more interwoven and unifying systems.

Light and Energy

Eternal energies move in waves. Invisible energy waves, valued by scientists and healers alike, can transverse certain materials such as crystal. Heat and electricity are obvious examples. Originally, handmade radios were known as crystal sets because they were constructed around the transmitting qualities of crystals.

Hit one hard enough and you see a spark. By forcing electricity out, you create light. Light can, similarly, be passed through a prism to create colours. The linked bands of colour composing a rainbow occur when white light shines through millions of drops of water to reveal its essence, pure colour.

Bo Jeffares Sekine, Vortex

Photons of light might be seen as building blocks containing blueprints for forming matter. Light, or illumination, can be used as a source of measurement. The speed at which light waves travel is constant – thus the Horse Head Nebula is about one light year tall. Each element reacts with or can be used to interpret the next. As Velasquez suggested in *The Spinners* everything is interwoven.

Threads of thought enter the fabric of our shared consciousness. Eyes and webs provide archetypal symbols for visionary understanding and flexible creativity. Fibre optics links old ideas about threads and vision to define a more up-to-date method of communication.

An electron can be either a particle or a wave. In essence the cosmos, All-That-Is (or however you define it) can, therefore, be interpreted simultaneously as either substance or flux; matter or movement. We ourselves, like wavelengths defined by physics, may be seen as physical bodies, 'overcoats for the soul', or eternal energy sources.

Light waves can be used to gauge speed in a cosmic context or, directed into lasers to cut cataracts or restore vision. Light can be collected into solar panels to create electric energy. Light energy moves mirrors in space reflecting back images of earlier astronomy.

Whereas in the past faith supported belief in unseen realities, science is catching up. Previously derided theories metamorphose into accepted dogma. Formerly outlandish ideas develop into accepted actualities. Science fiction (a genre with no limits) allows people to mentally explore and rehearse any scenario. The ability to duplicate individuals, hinted at by Huxley in *Brave New World* (1932), anticipates cloning experiments.

Genetic modifications allow us to mix and match human and animal combinations, transforming previous fantasies about metamorphoses into hard facts.

Body energies are traditionally checked and calmed by Chinese acupuncturists. Like traffic cops dealing with built up congestion or mad speeding, they try to stimulate an easy flow of energy. A build-up of stress (leading to pain) or sluggishness (leading to stagnation) equals dis-ease. Just as an easy flow of blood through veins and arteries is ideal, so a smooth flow of electro-magnetic energy is equally vital. Chinese doctors in the old days were supposed to keep you well. If they didn't, you didn't pay them, or (if powerful) got them killed. With a practical system like this they obviously tried very hard. These doctors made sophisticated body maps to chart our intrinsic power lines. Web imagery comes into play again to evoke these invisible channels called 'meridians'.

Chinese acupuncturists use the term *jing luo*. *Jing* means 'going through', as well as 'a thread in a fabric.' *Luo* means 'something which attaches or connects like a net'. Our network of invisible energy lines run through nodes stimulated for optimal health. These are like the pivotal junctions and roundabouts punctuating our roadways. Chinese doctors treat these points with needles, the Japanese with hand pressure. Indian *Ayurvedic* practitioners, or crystal healers create crystal 'webs' around bodies and places, utilising similar knowledge, practicing similar awareness.

Our bodies' meridians parallel the earth's energy grids. Where these invisible ley lines cross (or transverse hidden factors such as underground streams) they are often physically marked by ancient stone circles or later churches. Such structures celebrated natural power points appreciated by people intuitively aware of earth energies. Modern dowsers investigate these energy patterns. And, just as one can 'tune in' to a particular wavelength on the radio, so it is possible to learn to 'tune in' to other energy levels whether in people or places.

The fact that we do not physically see infra red and ultra violet does not mean that they do not exist. We get sunburnt. In the past, sound waves were used to tumble the walls of Jericho. Sound waves inaudible to humans can now be used for scanning foetuses in the womb, repairing eye lenses, or summoning dogs.

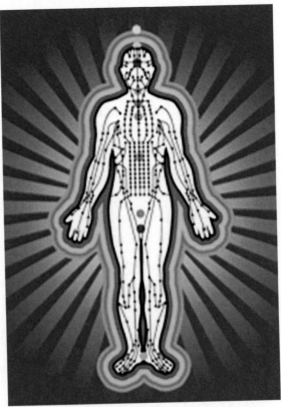

Meridians: invisible energy channels

Electro-magnetic impulses exist around us and move through us. We generate them. We contribute to the overall interchange of energy. Our emotions colour the atmosphere. We 'see red' when angry and we 'feel blue' when sad. Our bodies generate faint electromagnetic impulses. When a recording of the Earth's faint magnetic hum was played to disorientated spacemen, they felt reassured and consequently slept much better.

Auras, originally categorised by Kirlian photography, are now sanctified by science. This technique, pioneered in communist Russia, records non-material energies, like seven extra outer skins. These are often seen as red nearest the body, expanding out in a layered rainbow like expansions. They fluctuate according our moods and intent, as with the strongly-coloured force fields emanating from an effective healer's hands. Electric shocks reactivate hearts. X-rays and magnetic impulses are employed to 'see' the bones and soft tissues deep within our bodies, also be explored by miniature cameras exploring our inner landscapes. Thumb prints, acting as a signature in the past, are being replaced by biochemical analysis and genealogical profiling. We are now recognised by the constituents of our DNA.

Reflexologists can decode someone's inner tensions while carefully massaging their feet. Iridologists explore someone's overall health by observing the complexities marked out within the iris of their eyes, practical methods of inspecting the 'mirrors of the soul'. And, just as body language reflects passing reactions, so deeper and more constant pains reveal ingrained attitudes – whether chips on the shoulder, or pains in the arse. The positive side of this is that we can (in theory) learn to cultivate optimistic attitudes, develop 'mind over matter,' raise pain thresholds and so boost flagging immune systems.

We know the moon exerts a magnetic pull on the world's tides. Its gravitational influence on our oceans is easily observed. Swimming against the tide, we can physically feel this natural energy. We harness the tides to sail or glide. We increasingly capture wind and wave power. We can also be recognised by our personal sound waves or our voice patterns. So is it any coincidence that when we feel in emotional harmony with someone else we speak of being 'on the same wavelength', or describe inspirational breakthroughs as 'brainwaves'?

Scale and value are subjective. From fearing to fall off the edge of the world in the past, we are now cooped up in a global village. TV comedies with titles such as *Third Rock from the Sun* confirmed our position in spatial suburbia; commemorating the newfound modesty of a race once vain enough to consider itself the centre of everything.

We are composed of star dust, and our (present) home has always moved through space as a changing entity. Sensitive scientists make people aware that we are a part of a living ecosystem. Her weather patterns, changing coastlines, and supported species can all be affected by our ideas about life.

In Ancient Egypt, when the life-giving sun was worshipped as a deity, artists created a benign image. A round sun had many rays concluding in small, outstretched human hands. Human and space imagery combined in this easily assimilated symbol of blessing, placed protectively over golden depictions of the Pharaoh's family. Golden yellow is traditionally associated with sunlight (and the solar plexus chakra) just as green is associated with nature and growth. Our symbolic use of the colour green as a descriptive term (as in Prospero's reference to his 'verdure' or inner energy) now takes on a wider meaning. This colour now signifies environmental awareness and planetary concern.

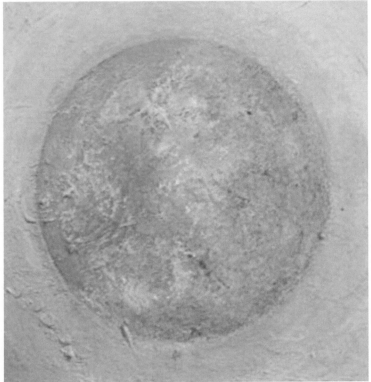

Bo Jeffares Sekine, Small World

Everyone has their shaman-like moments, when they can intuitively sense or reveal hidden truths, or in Klee's phrase 'render' or 'make visible'. An inventive artist/scientist like Leonardo da Vinci described painting as a thing of the mind. He could produce an imaginative image of a cataclysmic, whirlpool-like deluge, as though seeing it from high above as we easily can from our modern aircraft and satellites. In the Space Age we learn to see our changing environment objectively from outside: we appreciate its interwoven blues and greens, burnt patches, fragile pale clouds, opaline effects and vulnerability.

New Horizons?

The Tempest focused on exploration of Brave New Worlds like Shakespeare's enchanted isle. And now our technical acceleration is such that global scientists are planning for people to go to Mars and contemplating colonial space cities, like those already envisaged in science fiction, a genre always one step ahead.

People living in space, without gravity, would grow differently. Their bones and muscles would be subject to radical alterations. They would also be born without our temporal and climatic heritage. Accepted rhythms balancing day with night, and all the emotions associated with seasonal changes (which we take for granted) would evaporate.

These beings would be the first humans to develop in a new arena completely detached from all our old, intellectual landscape symbols which earlier generations have lovingly honed and polished. Our archetypal metaphors for exploring existence could become cultural myths, fading racial memories. Wouldn't these people's everyday sense of scale, spatial values and consequent sense of relativity be way beyond our comprehension?

Will we eventually evolve into citizens of the cosmos? And how will our interpretations of matter and dark matter manifest in multiple dimensions?

What kind of maps will we make in the future? Maps tell us as much about map-makers as what they try to define. The Inuit, for example, fish hazardous coastal waters. They create indented wooden maps to help them feel and recall the relative distances between the intricacies of their coastlines by day or night. Navigational aids with two practical advantages, these maps can be felt in the dark, and can also float if accidentally dropped overboard. The land, being largely irrelevant, was left blank.

So it is with all maps. Whatever you don't value or believe in is irrelevant and therefore left out, as when the apartheid-era South African government 'forgot' to mark black townships. What you don't care about is literally a waste of space. Prosaic tunnels and crossings on our world maps could be replaced by tomorrow's time warps and worm holes. Factors which our limited minds currently class as fantasy, or have yet to envisage, could well be mapped out as part of tomorrow's boring actuality. As it is, searching maps for information online, we provide the matrix with as much data as we receive.

Dots, smudges and swirls appear to be the basic visual impressions given in the latest highly technical, scientific portrayals of outer space. Aboriginal artists have portrayed star clusters coherently simply using dots and lines for millennia. Similarly, mandalas can still be built up from a series of coloured, concentric circles designed to focus the mind and thus evoke the infinite. A Zen master portrayed the whole cosmos with a single circular brush stroke. A parallel is found in the poet Henry Vaughan's simple image:

> I saw Eternity the other night
> Like a great Ring of pure and endless light

Seeking a design for a cenotaph for the great physicist Newton, the eighteenth-century French architect Boullée conceived a plan like an upturned colander. His design, puncturing a dome with holes in the positions of the stars to let in natural light and suggest the heavens was basic. Simple images make powerful symbols. Van Gogh's starry skies have an emotional intensity hard to match with impersonal, technological data. Perhaps the most vital images are those which retain the ability to provoke not only curiosity but also a sense of wonder.

Simple things are easy to understand. Bees make honey. Spiders spin. Sufi mystics equate the spiders' ability to spin silken cords with their own ability to physically spin around. They twirl themselves into a trance hoping to become channels for divine love. Spiders' inbuilt skills make them into archetypal creative symbols. They feature in contexts as varied as the Arachne myth, the tale of King Robert the Bruce, or the Nazca spider.

Some Native Americans believe the song can sing the singer. They believe a poetic image or song exists in its own right, and can sometimes come to someone in a dream or ceremony, demanding to be sung. Similarly, some Western composers such as Mozart have dreamt of marvellous music which they rushed to remember and note down on waking. Dreams and intuitive hunches inspire us all, and add to our creative repertoire. Sometimes they are consciously sought, as when Native Americans copy spiders' webs to make symbolic nets called 'Dream Catchers'.

There are many examples of art and individuals becoming so fused that it is hard to tell one from the other, as with Yeats' question 'How can I tell the dancer from the dance?' Degas produced studies of young ballet dancers resting, practising and training to personify music and movement through dance performances. In visual works, Degas provides a creative analogy with a dancer's tireless dedication, enacting cycles of vision and revision, to embody aesthetic perfection.

Degas stated blandly that he wished to paint women as cats. Fat chance. The latter always remain elegant: they have more bones in their spines. The painter's meaning was probably more prosaic: unadulterated by overt sentimentality, he wished to use women's bodies as raw materials for his artistic experiments.

Zola compared the Impressionist's vision of life with angles of nature seen through a temperament. One's temperament, like a pair of rose coloured spectacles (or tinted contact lenses) colours one's vision, alters one's interpretation of reality. Coloured shades have medicinal value. Blue light cures jaundiced babies. Picture-makers reveal their personalities not only in their choice of subject matter but also by their preferred palette.

Artists are thieves. Picasso admired Velazquez. Wishing to absorb, or assimilate, the earlier Spaniard's compositional subtleties, he deliberately set about dissecting *The Spinners* like a calculating butcher disjointing a carcass, or a mechanic dismantling an engine to find out what makes it tick, or a detective investigating a crime scene. Like professional code breakers, artists unravel an admired teacher's illusions before trying to go one further.

Francis Bacon, the nihilistic English painter, was equally fascinated by Velazquez's subtleties. He seized upon the masked repression inherent in many of Velazquez's potent figureheads. Beaten in childhood, shocked by war deaths, Bacon selected an image of an already isolated figure to encage or isolate it still further. He adapted Velazquez's poised Pope in an enclosed room. It becomes a tortured, screaming figure trapped within a spatial grid. His raw *Study after Velazquez's Portrait of Pope Innocent* (1953) encapsulates his personal feelings of fear and its reverse, aggression.

Bo Jeffares Sekine, Chakra Man

Bacon's psychological state informed his visual transformations. So, too, in a different medium, did those of the Italian film director Antonioni. This film-maker's desire for passion made him place a red filter over his camera lens in 1964 while filming his metaphysical masterpiece *The Red Desert*, a film about sexual passion..

In holistic medicine all around the world each individual's heart, mind and spirit energies are demonstrated by the current state of their physical bodies. The combined clarity and brightness of their chakras, or energy centres, elucidate their overall well-being. These areas of specific evolution work up from the red root or base chakra to white at the highest crown chakra. Our lower, egotistical red/orange/yellow range and our higher more creative blue/purple/indigo range are linked through a green, central heart chakra.

A holistic healer often 'sees' or interprets bodies in terms of pure energy. Dark areas in the aura may reveal problems, such as negative after effects from shock, before they have started to materialise as physical imbalances. Emotional stress forming the root of a problem can then be acknowledged and cures sought for pain and suffering. The fact that placebos can work reveals how beliefs create reality. Trusting relationships with any doctors and an implicit belief in all their skills help to place us on a sure road to recovery.

Food for Thought:
What's Real for You?

Each individual's emotional qualities colour their relationships. Similarly, their mental attitudes govern their 'feedback' from their life experiences.

Metaphysical ideas often involve food. Perhaps solid food imagery grounds intellectual ideas or spices them up? Economic ratios become palatable when described domestically as 'pie charts'. Language transforms food for survival into food for thought. Physical health experts state we are what we eat, but the Buddha wisely noted: 'All that we are is a result of what we have thought'.

Edible imagery helps us process facts. The millions of white stars comprising the 'Milky Way' provide a good example. Surely any vast galaxy feels friendlier and more acceptable when associated with our first source of nourishment? 'Star-struck' lovers are said to be 'spaced out', or on 'cloud nine' or 'over the moon'. The image of a honeymoon gives honey's earthy sweetness a spatial twist, placing it in an extra-terrestrial context. Blending sugary honey with the magnetic powers of the moon marries mystery and sensuality, or suggests a good month on mead. Another blend of food and space – the phrase 'pie in the sky' – sums up fantasies about imagining future 'just desserts.'

Why do we use culinary language to say a computer has bytes or a menu? Why do quarks have 'flavours'? Why do we describe one of science's major breakthroughs as 'quantum soup'? By making this part of a great 'kitchen sink drama', cross-fertilising cookery and cosmology, science and soup, we bring the infinite down to earth. Quantum soup sounds fun. It is easily acknowledged, accepted and swallowed, as the human mind mentally digests new information.

People, places and situations are frequently compared with food. The tempting city of New York is described as the big apple. A reliable person is described as 'a good egg' or 'the salt of the earth'. Young hopefuls are told 'the world's your oyster'. And in 'nuttier' moments we are all 'one sandwich short of a picnic'.

Physical and metaphysical meanings overlap when we 'feast our eyes'. Basho, the Japanese poet praised for expressing universal truths in minimal (often onomatopoeic) form, loved nature with philosophic detachment. His comment on hearing he had been burgled is typical: the thief cannot steal the moonlight from my window. This transcendental approach to reality is captured in his famous frog *haiku*, where a frog leaps into an old green well, implicitly creating ever expanding circles of ripples which stretch out over its surface.

Basho's classic example of cause and effect has an aesthetic parallel in the extended sand 'waves' carefully raked around the rock 'islands' in Zen gardens. We see similar results when a boat leaves a wake, a plane produces vapour, a meteorite leaves a fire tail, or a joke creates ripples of laughter. Each incident, or person, affects the next. Quantum physicists are now approaching the idea that we all actively influence our environment. So the personality of each scientific investigator seems to have a bearing on their logical investigations. Is science becoming subjective?

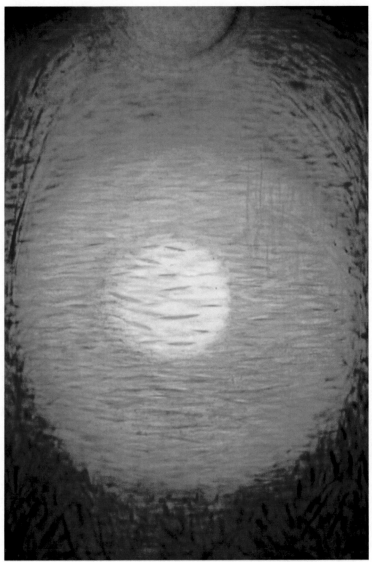

Bo Jeffares Sekine, Moon Reflected on Green Water

Just as each scientist's energetic qualities impact on their work, so do the most powerful invisible qualities such as love and compassion. No man is an island. Awareness of emotional intelligence and emotional boundaries can help us to envisage change. Sharing the earth peaceably is a huge spatial challenge. Your current take on reality defines how you perceive your body space, dwelling space, work space, communal space and how you currently 'see' your life. How do you conceive our planet's place within the solar system, galaxy, universe and cosmos?

Where you cut off, or connect, is up to you. But think about it because by defining space, you are really defining your own reality.

Bo Jeffares Sekine, Central Target

Many writers experiment with the imaginative possibilities of game space. The author J.K. Rowling tests her young wizard, Harry Potter, in a spatially complex game (brilliantly realised in film). She thus provides this child hero with extra challenges, extra power and extra magical potential.

Where most school stories highlight sporting and bullying incidents set on a school playing fields or sports grounds, Rowling goes one further. Her protagonist competes with darker and more devious opponents in a much more remarkable setting. The three dimensional space for the magical game of Quiddich provides a unique stage for Harry to demonstrate his skills on a broomstick, his physical and tactical triumphs. His amazed audience below, plus every reader and film-goer, sees him excel in a spectacular arena, capable of blending 'real' with 'surreal' elements within one compact field of action.

A space outsider puts our world in sharp perspective in *La Belle Verte* (1996). In this provocative film Corline Serreau's sensitive alien is shocked by the greed and materialism ruining our earth. Contrasts with her own nature loving home, the Green Planet, point up our human imbecilities. This comedy with a message was banned by the European Union.

Earlier cultures adapted microcosmic game spaces to teach moral lessons. Native Americans invented a game for children called 'Snakes and Ladders.' It demonstrates cause and effect. Players cast dice before climbing up a ladder or sliding down a snake. The basic message is be good or you will suffer. In this game 'snakes' are synonymous with feeling down, behaving badly and experiencing sudden 'falls from grace'. We automatically associate 'ladders' with uplifting themes. 'Study' leads up the educational ladder to knowledge. 'Pride' comes before a fall. Positive virtues create uplifting results in a game which illustrates how what goes around comes around.

A target helps us focus. Surrounded by rings of concentric circles, a central target aids concentration. It is versatile and can be adapted for playful darts, killer arrows or company strategies. A target can symbolically centre aims and ambitions. Playing with these themes, wondering what children would enjoy, I painted an old lid and called it *Central Target*. This centralised rainbow disc combines moveable magnets, wires and attachable objects. The original version has been gifted with hearts, keys, bells and feathers – small personal treasures and symbols – added by people playing with ideas about life in a safe symbolic space.

Game Space allows us to work out old obsessions and form new strategies. Lust for dominance, for example, is traditionally played out on chess boards which are like miniature battle fields. Traditionally, chess pieces represent a set command structure. There is an authoritarian power pyramid of royalty, knights, castles and bishops which combine secular authority with religious prestige. Dominant pieces are usually larger and more intricately carved. Powerful figures have their own, unique ways of moving across the board. These political heavyweights are fronted by smaller, identical pieces, cannon fodder, unimportant, easily replaced 'pawns in the game'.

It is significant that during the twentieth century Cold War between the USSR and the West chess championships were an integral part of the political scene. Duels between clashing adversaries were dramatically staged, like age-old instances of single combat designed to settle national conflicts. Each side tried to demonstrate their superior intelligence and strategies on these small but highly publicised game fields.

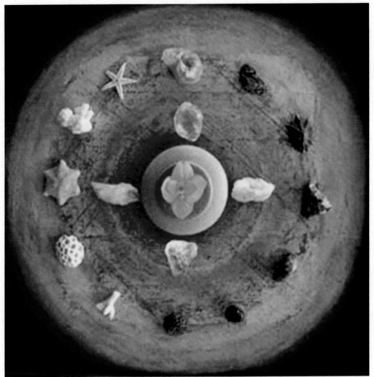

Bo Jeffares Sekine, Green Centre

Green Centre is an adaptation of a traditional chess board. Hopefully the emphasis shifts from a stage for destructive fighting to a unifying symbol putting nature first. How can we visualise new formats to suggest a more appreciative world order? Here a traditional black and white grid is transformed into a greeny-blue circular design, earth and sky colours. The human power structure has been replaced by a circle of natural, organic pieces. Crystals and corals symbolise land and sea. Living leaves take centre stage. This is an example of a small image trying to transmit a big idea.

How would you encapsulate change? What would your creative equivalent be? Even if chess is played within three dimensional space, as it can be, it still relies on old, well-established power symbols. How would you practically or poetically update these old symbols to try to change our emotional focus?

Would your power pyramid include multinationals and the media? What would your representative scale of human reference span, from personal friends to global citizens? Would your choices include quixotic players, like the wise fools enlivening Tarot cards and Shakespearian plays? Would you have a joker in your pack? How would you move, eliminate, amalgamate and ultimately win? And what does this say about you and your current worldview?

Which symbols would you adapt to clarify our planetary problems? Circles and spheres suggest unity. Squares and cubes imply order. Triangles and pyramids point up aspiration. Colours evoke feelings. Roads of life reveal directions. Bridges make connections. Trees describe growth. The sun generates heat and light and the moon adds mystery and magic. Together the sun and moon create a sequence of seasonal rhythms to inspire our own cyclical celebrations providing celestial constants in a material world.

Emotive images form part of our heritage. We experiment with them to define reality. We use them to reflect on our relationship with the earth and our pivotal roles as earth artists:

cloud	transience	angel	spirituality
wave	energy	star	inspiration
rock	duration	spiral	evolution
dragonfly	metamorphosis	circle	peace
spider	creativity	square	logic
web	communication	triangle	ambition
tree	growth	heart	emotion
seed	idea	eye	visionary scope
fruit	achievement	foot	physical impact

Carbon footprints refer to our impact on the environment as we destroy our surroundings showing more greed than sense. Spatial hunger evolves into spatial starvation. People fight for living space. The earth's surface spaces plus all the treasures above and below the land and sea are up for grabs.

How can we learn to become more self-aware? How can we redefine crucial approaches to reality? How do we instigate change? The surrealists juggled incongruities, making visual jokes to stimulate critical reappraisals. Could this experimental approach be one way forward, shaking up our ideas to permit new leaps of faith, rethinking life?

What's Real for You? ('just one I made earlier') is a frivolous adaptation of the Eastern game of *Go* which is dedicated to winning space. Wondering how children sense space and perceive reality, I replaced traditional black and white discs with a colourful collection of found and fabricated objects. These include toys, sweets and children's building blocks. Moving on from the aim of gaining two dimensional space, to ideas of inhabiting and moving through different kinds of space, toy cats, fishes and birds represent walking, swimming and flying. Cars and snails also indicate earthly travel while implying some of its restrictions. Stars and angels evoke unbounded dimensions –such as astronomers' Deep Field Space and spiritualists' Meditational Space.

Bo Jeffares Sekine, What's Real for You?

Angels, divine messengers in many religions, function in any spheres. Balancing these intangible beings are 'real' down-to-earth foods, crab apples and walnuts, prized as natural remedies. Psychological experiences unrestricted by logical or material boundaries are suggested by an organic combination of a poppyhead, brain coral and a calcified wormhole. This wormhole evokes a worm's modest, earthbound 'expeditions' but also conjures up wilder adventures spinning new webs out through time and space.

> We play with pictures to explore the future.
> Personal evolution is an imaginative game.

List of Illustrations

All measurements in centimetres

Index